We Shall Live in Heaven

By Harri Haamer

Tartu Academy of Theology

We Shall Live in Heaven
By
Harri Haamer

Translated by Tiina Kaia Ets

We Shall Live In Heaven has been translated and published in the following languages:
1990 Finnish
1993 Estonian
2000 Russian
2007 German
2007 English
Danish (Translated but not yet published)

Cover design and background photo by Jerry Pitmon

Ebook Format by OÜ Flagella

ISBN 978-9949-9931-3-0
ISBN 978-9949-9931-0-9 (pdf)
ISBN 978-9949-9931-1-6 (epub)
ISBN 978-9949-9931-2-3 (mobi)

www.tatest.org

We Shall Live in Heaven
By Harri Haamer

Table of Contents

ACKNOWLEDGEMENTS

Cordial thanks go to Tiina Kaia Ets, who translated this book from the original Estonian into English. She did this as a labor of love, in honor of Pastor Harri Haamer.

All the profits from the sale of this book will go toward the education of clergy and pastoral care givers in Estonia. If you would like to make a donation to support mission work in Estonia you are welcome to find options from tatest.org.

FOREWORD

My father, Harri Haamer (July 8, 1906–August 8, 1987), was born in the small town of Kuressaare on the green island Saaremaa which nestles up against Estonia, just out in the Baltic Sea. He was the middle son among three in the family, and he grew up in that peaceful place.

He did not know it, but before he was born, a book had been written whose influence would fling him across the vast continent of Eurasia and into a wretched exile. That book was Karl Marx's *The Communist Manifesto*, and its ideas still enslave whole populations, as it did millions during the Soviet time. Harri was only 11 when the Bolshevik Revolution seized power in Russia. He was 12 when his homeland, which had been a Russian colony for 200 years, took advantage of the upheaval and won independence.

At age 16 he became a Boy Scout and later was a Scout leader, beginning a life-long calling to care for youth. After graduation from the Gymnasium (high school) he entered studies with the Faculty of Theology at the University of Tartu, from which he graduated in 1929. He was ordained a Lutheran pastor and appointed to Püha (Holy) Congregation in Saaremaa. In the autumn of 1933, he was called to Paulus Church in Tartu.

He married Maimu Maramaa on May 10, 1934, and they were blessed with three children, Eenok, Maarja and Andres. However, turmoil surrounded their little home and parish, as first the Soviet Russians invaded Estonia, and then in 1941 the Nazis (Fascists). 1944 the Soviet Russians game back and stayed for almost 50 years.

A fire burnt down the Paulus Church in 1944. When the WWII was over 1945, my father started to restore this church. The Soviet Occupation

Authorities did not favor it, and neither did they like his pastoral activities with students. On February 5, 1948, Harri was arrested and deported to a convict-labor camp in far eastern Siberia. He was sentenced to eight years in concentration camps because he was accused of having educated Estonian youth in the wrong spirituality. Here his book begins.

Not content to strike at him alone, his family was also scheduled to be deported to Siberia on March 25, 1949. On that day, more than 20,000 Estonians were forced to leave their homes for Siberia. Most of them never returned, and we also might have gone and died there. Andres was six, Maarja ten, and I was 13 years old.

However, our mother got word of it and decided that we would leave home before the soldiers came. Andres had caught a high fever, and mother had to leave him with neighbors. My sister Maarja was taken to people we knew. So began a six-anda-half year period of escaping and hiding ourselves constantly. Mother, a 17-year-old homeless boy named Albert whom we had adopted, and I became "anti-Communist partisans" in the dense forests of Southern Estonian. It was possible to hide ourselves there because faithful local people, who knew us, helped us and risked their freedom for us. For four of those six years we lived in an underground bunker dug adjacent to a farm cellar. The kindly couple who lived there fed us, cared for us, and even vented the bunker's chimney through theirs.

God twice saved us from getting arrested. Once a raid was conducted on the farm where we were sheltered, and the soldiers almost caught us. However, they did not recognize us as the Haamer family, supposedly a mother with a young teenage boy, a little girl and a small boy. Next, when they came to capture us somewhere else, we were there but God closed their eyes so that they did not see the door of our room.

I fell ill with bone tuberculosis, and there was no way to treat it. We could not go to the doctor, since we could not be seen in public. Danger was everywhere. God heard our prayers and the disease withdrew, so that I was able to grow up, do my work and take care of my family. This time became for me a university of suffering, which mirrored the anguish and darkness in my country. It was then, when I was fourteen, that God called me to become His servant.

I was 20 when my father returned from Siberia and gathered together his scattered family. It was due to the great mercy of God that we were all alive. We received the gift of life with father for 32 more years, and those were blessed years. Father was a profound believer, who trusted Jesus completely. His great influence is also reflected in our children. My three sons have studied theology, and they all have become workers for God's Kingdom. They are lutheran pastors of the third generation.

Father Harri has also had a great impact on the Estonian Lutheran Church. His mind was open ecumenically, and he tried to unite all those who loved God. He had many friends in different Christian churches. I also consider the Tartu Academy of Theology, which I founded, to be my father's heritage.

He was an excellent story teller and a skilled writer. His literary heritage is large, and a special place is dedicated to the spiritual literature he wrote for children. Out of his approximately 2,000 preserved sermons, there are two published collections. Through his blessed heritage he is still talking to the people of his beloved Estonia.

Eenok Haamer
Son of Harri Haamer
Founder of Tartu Academy of Theology

INTRODUCTION

Harri Haamer, the pastor of St. Paul's congregation in Tartu, was arrested in the winter of 1948. He was taken to the main prison in Tallinn, as preparation for a long trip to the Kolyma Gulag in far-eastern Siberia. In the summer of 1948, he was sentenced and deported to an eight-year term in a labor camp and an additional three-year term of "limited freedom". The prisoner's sentence was shortened by two years for his diligent work but upon leaving the Gulag, Haamer was told that he faced "lifelong exile". This was eventually reversed in 1955 when he was notified that he had been "arrested in error". Such was Haamer's account in his 1974 New Year's sermon (published in a collection of sermons by Estonians *Tie, totuus, elämä (*The way, the truth, the life*)* Kirjaneliö 1990). Stalin had died in 1953, ushering in a period of thaw; a chapter in USSR's and occupied Estonia's history had ended.

Harri Haamer was permitted to continue his ministry upon his return from Siberia. However, the convicted pastor was not permitted to resume at his former congregation but was instead sent to Tarvastu in eastern Estonia. He ministered there from 1955 until his death in 1987. He passed away on August 8th, 1987 at the age of 81.

Haamer's ministry was exceptionally long considering that he had been installed as pastor nearly two years ahead of the established age limit of 25. Due to Estonia's severe shortage of pastors, he was permitted to minister until his 80's, despite the retirement cutoff of 70. He served the church for 58 years.

Harri Haamer was born July 8, 1906 in Kuressaare, Saaremaa. Like his brother Eerik Haamer, a noteworthy painter, Harri was artistically gifted;

multi-talented in sports, he was also a promising decathlete. But Haamer's true passion was for youth work and becoming a Scout and youth leader. After high school, he began studying for the ministry.

At 22, Harri Haamer completed his theological studies at Tartu University and was appointed into the newly established position as Secretary of Youth Ministries. This appointment lasted only six months until the autumn of 1929 when he was encouraged to apply as pastor to Saaremaa's Püha-congregation, which had languished long without a minister. Haamer was installed as pastor in October of 1929. In 1933, he transferred from Püha to St. Paul's congregation in Tartu. He served at St. Paul's for fifteen years which included the German occupation and war years. As the Germans withdrew in August of 1944, amid fierce battles over Tartu, a fire destroyed St. Paul's church, congregational house and Haamer's home.

Harri Haamer was renowned as a great storyteller and a friend of children. He published three short, self-illustrated books of children's stories in 1937-38. His most expansive publication was a 144-page devotional titled *Tema käsi* (His Hand, 1934). Another devotional intended for young people called *Sinule* (For You) appeared in 1939, followed by a short novel *Ester* (Esther) during the German occupation in 1943. The ensuing Soviet occupation ended a promising publishing venture though Haamer did not stop writing, as this collection of remembrances attests. The 1991 Estonian hymnal contains over twenty hymns either written or translated by Harri Haamer. During his time in Tarvastu, he continued his studies and attained a master's degree in theology in 1962. He was an Old Testament and Hebrew lecturer at Tallinn's theological institute.

Estonia's short-lived 20-year independence ended in the summer of 1940. The Soviet armies invaded Estonia in June and by August, USSR had annexed Estonia, the ramifications of the Molotov-Ribbentrop agreement, a non-aggression pact between USSR and Hitler's Germany (August 8, 1939) which included a secret codicil assigning the Baltics and Finland to the Soviets, which ignited Finland's Winter War.

House searches, arrests and deportations to Siberia began immediately upon Soviet occupation. Approximately 7,000 were imprisoned in 1940. June 14th, 1941 marked the mass-deportation of over 10,000 Estonians who were forcibly removed from their homesteads – men were sent into labor-camps, the women & children to Siberia. Germany declared war on the Soviet Union in the summer of 1941 and invaded the Baltics. German occupation continued until 1944, when around 70,000 Estonians fled to the West in fear of the returning Soviets. Thousands of men – including Estonian soldiers wishing to avoid being drafted into the German army – hid themselves in the forests in order to prepare for resistance. These "forest brothers" maintained their guerilla tactics until the mid-50's, and the remaining forest brothers did not emerge until the 70's.

The imprisonment and deportation of those deemed as enemies of the State resumed in the old fashion, "in all silence but in greater numbers" (Mart Laar). It is estimated that about 10,000 were arrested and killed annually until the end of March, 1949, which marked a sweeping mass-deportation. This was designed to intimidate the citizens into joining collectives which had been forcibly imposed on all farms and homesteads. According to official reports, well over 20,000 Estonians were banished on March 25th, 1949. The actual number was easily double that, and according to some reports, even greater. The Haamer family avoided this fate by hiding from the authorities for long periods of time.

Nothing comparable to this happened again after Stalin's death. But an atmosphere of crippling fear and mistrust enveloped all and did not dissipate until the late 1980's when freedom's winds began to blow. The autocratic communist party feared potential opponents who in turn feared their rulers. One could never be certain who might turn out to be an informant; apprehension and helplessness prevailed. Democratic freedoms were severely limited and human rights were routinely violated. The State consistently spread suspicion which worked like a poison among the people. Society had become sick.

Harri Haamer was by no means the only Estonian Lutheran pastor to suffer deportation and forced labor. Between 1940 and '41, 17 fulltime pastors were deported to Siberia of whom only a couple eventually returned. Likewise, practically the same number of pastors shared this fate between 1944 and '54, but nearly all of them returned home and resumed their ministries, some as early as 1955, several in 1956. The church's activities were strictly controlled: worship and religious services within the church building, as well as, funerals were permitted. All other activities were forbidden:

youth- and children's ministries, religious education, diaconate services, publishing, and all contact with sister-churches abroad. Within a decade, the church had lost two-thirds of its pastors either due to flight, banishment, deportations, or executions. Of the roughly 220 pastors serving in 1939, only about 70 remained by 1949, leaving half the existing congregations without a pastor.

In February 1988, the Estonian Heritage Preservation Association (Eesti Muinsuskaitse Selts) launched a massive collection of the Estonians' written memories and recorded accounts; a project intended to save and preserve a precious history from destruction. The widely-publicized project was a tremendous success, yielding an abundance of material. Recollections and documents of the 1941 deportation were published in Finnish, in 1989, under the title *Kesäkuun 14. Päiva* (Fourteenth of June). Harri Haamer's personal recollections have also been preserved in this collection.

Though Haamer's diaries do not add anything substantively new to the already published works about life and conditions in Soviet prison-camps, their significance lies in something else. While taking the reader through Estonia's bitter tribulations and painful memories, his accounts testify of the sustaining power of a Christian's faith and hope. As Harri Haamer would affirm – while imitating the arrogant intonations of the prison guards – "Hopelessness has no place in *Our* program."

Translated by Maarit Vaga from Tauno Väinola's Introduction to the Finnish edition 1990.

THE JOURNEY BEGINS

I am arrested. They don't talk with me very long in the "gray house" of Tartu. The same pock-marked *chekist*[1] who had been waving his Nagant revolver around on the street sends me down to the cellar. There, two guards with *Komsomol*[2] insignia order me to disrobe. "Why must I do that?" I ask.

"Are you in jail for the first time?" asks one young man.

"For the first time!" I reply.

"How old are you?" asks the same boy.

"Nearly forty-two."

He turns to the other one and says: "This guy has lived on this earth for forty two years, and he's in jail for the first time!"

At the time, I do not understand why they should be so surprised.

What else can I do but strip myself naked? They take my belt. They cut off my pants buttons. They pull out my shoelaces. They empty my pockets. They take my Testament. They take my money. They like my pocket knife. One of them says that they won't be recording this one. He slides my pocket knife into his own pocket as I look on.

When they order me to get dressed once again, I have to hold my pants up with one hand, because I have nothing to fasten them with. Then they shove me into a cell.

There I stand. Not even a stool to sit on. I could sit on the floor, if I pull my knees up tight to my chin. I have never been in such a miserable

---

1 *chekist* – Communist secret police agent (KGB)

2 *Komsomol* – Young Communist League; membership was required of all young people

chamber. A 15-watt bulb burns in the ceiling. The space is too small to take even a single step.

Why have they thrown me in here? I see there have been others here before me. They have used something to scrape their names into the plaster. But another hand has erased them.

One name remains: Laine Aller. She has suffered in this cell before me. Perhaps she was taken away yesterday, perhaps today, right before I got here. Is she a young girl, or perhaps a mother? I wonder what she did to make them arrest her. I have never heard the name before, but I will remember it for a long time. It means that she stood here, just like I am standing, with just enough presence of mind to scrape her name into the wall. I wonder what she scraped with. They take away all your sharp objects. Perhaps they left her one button, perhaps the clasp of her bra. Or maybe she scraped it with her fingernail? I ponder my own situation. Why have they arrested me? I was shown no arrest warrant. They entrapped me. That woman called herself Olenina. The city's Executive Committe Secretary was Olenina. But was she also an officer for state security? Have Beria's police finally recruited all the officials into their service? Is the Executive Committee a branch of the state security apparatus? They had wanted to honor me by granting me the job of informer. Perhaps my refusal to accept this "honor" is the reason for my arrest. I don't know; I really don't know anything. They just want to dispose of me quietly. A few weeks ago, the Deputy for Religious Affairs ordered me to stop conducting my youth classes, which were attended by many university students. I told him: "I won't stop. It is more important to obey the word of God than the word of man." He became angry and said: "Well, then we must find another way to discipline you." And now this is undoubtedly "another way to discipline me."

You see, the Deputy is also an agent for the state security apparatus. We are surrounded by Beria's police. What I did or did not do makes no difference; eventually, they would have found me.

My wife Maimu came along, as if trying to protect me. No sooner had we stepped out of our house than a Jewish boy began to follow us. He elbowed his way over to me and inquired, rolling his r's: "Are you Pastor Haamer?" I replied, "No, I'm not." But he shadowed me all the way to the "gray house." There I was met by an entire pack of men carrying pistols. I did not need to introduce myself to them. They quickly took me up the stairs, not letting us utter another word to each other.

Did they release Maimu? My son Eenok has a fever. I wanted to call the doctor. And now I am standing in this cell. I was in such a hurry to get here that I did not even take the time to pray with my children. Eenok called to me from his bed, but I simply glanced at him without realizing I should say good-bye. Maarja and Albert were in school, and Ats sat on the floor, playing with his blocks.

But all those who have despaired here before me had been torn away from someone. Whom did Laine leave behind? A father, a mother, a sister, a brother, a husband, her children? How could I ever find out? I had better pray for the loved ones she left behind. I pray for my children. I pray for Laine Aller's children, although I do not even know if she has any. Perhaps they apprehended her as she was taking food into the forest for her father or brother. Now she is being prosecuted as a "bandit collaborator." Bandits. How will my crime be classified?

I ponder my fate as well as Laine Aller's for a long time. I feel that if I ever meet her, I will greet her as a sister.

Suddenly, the door opens and a somber-faced guard wordlessly hands me a a bowl of gray soup. Its odor envelops the cell. Just as wordlessly, I push it back to him.

Nobody comes around to bother me any more.

The corridor gradually becomes silent. Perhaps it is already nighttime. But there is no way I can lie down.

I do not need to. Two uniformed men open the cell and order me to follow them. One officer walks ahead, the other behind, and the man with the machine gun carries my leather suitcase, which probably represents the fruits of their search. They have handcuffed me, just in case. But it is hard for me to move along, because my pants sag around my hips and my unlaced shoes want to flop off my feet.

The streets are empty. I am taken to the station. One of the drivers at the station recognizes me. I whisper to him to tell my wife that I am being taken away. But the *chekists* are already sending the man away.

For the first time in my life, I am traveling at the government's expense and under heavy guard. They have apprehended a dangerous national criminal. The *chekists* are diligently fulfilling their plan.

I AM TAKEN TO "INDIA"

If I take stock of everything I have learned of geography, I have some idea of what India is like. But I had no conception of the "India" that awaited me behind the door of Cell 17 of Patarei Prison. Only tales of fear and terror passed from cell to cell about this "India." For the most part, they did not concern political prisoners, because none of them were eligible for placement into this cell, which held a collection of the most loathsome cutthroats from the entire prison. Occasionally, the prison's fire brigade would be called in to subdue them with a stream of water sprayed in through the *kormushka*[3] ("fodder bin," an opening in the cell door through which food is passed). Whenever muted screams from somewhere at the end of the corridor echoed into our cell, I was certain they emanated from "India."

And then one night, not in a dream, but in reality, I stand at the door of Cell 17 and wait to be shoved inside.

How did this happen?

I spent a month in the Patarei Prison hospital. I had fallen victim to scurvy while being held in the cellar of the Pagari Street building. The Hebrew doctor treated me very humanely, and would not let them release me from the hospital until the abscesses on my legs had healed and my teeth no longer rattled loose in my gums.

Once out of the hospital, I am back with my people. Before long, we forge close friendships. I immediately begin leading evening prayers in the cell. I teach the men a beautiful song that has comforted me a great deal.

3 *kormushka* – "Fodder bin" the hole through which prisoners were fed.

It begins with the words "The light shall soon defeat the darkness, a time of joy shall follow our tears," and it ends with the comforting words "The beggar shall be wealthy, the prisoner shall be freed..."

Soon, the men are singing it with great enthusiasm. It is barely a week since I have begun providing spiritual comfort to my cellmates when an official wearing golden epaulettes bursts into the cell with his entourage and shouts, "Who's singing in here?"

I know that no one dares to tell him we are doing something as a group, because we would be in deep trouble; Soviet authorities fear organized resistance above all else. And so, before anyone else gets a chance to open his mouth, I calmly step forth and reply, "I am singing." "Why are you singing?" the officer asks angrily.

"I am a Christian and I am in prison. I must sing to keep sadness at bay. Christ's apostles Paul and Silas also sang in prison, so that they would not despair."

"All right, all right!" says the golden epaulette. He turns on his heel and disappears along with his entire entourage. A *korpusnoi*[4] (unit commander) shows up later to take my name. The next morning, I am summoned *s vestsami*[5] ("with all my things"). I am shoved into Cell 13. Some of the men there know me. Some of the others know me by way of the prison "telegraph system," which serves to transmit all the prison's news.

That very first night in my new cell, I begin fulfilling my obligations as a man of the cloth. I recite Bible passages from memory and explain them. I console and reassure my fellow sufferers with my sermons. Our prayer sessions are solemn and moving. Naturally, I teach them the same song.

But I fare no better in this cell. I am left in peace for about a week. Then one morning, the same gold-epauletted[6] official bursts into the cell. Now I realize that he is the prison's chief commander.

"Who's singing in here?" he shouts even more fiercely than before.

Once again, I step up to him and reply, "I am singing."

"You again!" the officer scolds.

---

4 *Korpusnoi* – Prison unit commander

5 *s vestsami* – "With your things;" an order for a prisoner to move out

6 *gold-epaulette* – Shoulder fringes on Communist Youth uniforms; this signified a higher rank

"Yes, I am a Christian and I am in prison. I must sing to keep sadness at bay. Paul and Silas were in prison..."

"All right, all right, I've already heard your sermon." The lord and master gives up in disgust.

My name is not written up this time. But the next morning, I hear the same order once more: "Come along, with all your things!"

For the third time in as many weeks, I find myself in a new cell. And I start all over again.

I feel as if "The light shall soon defeat the darkness" is becoming the anthem of the congregation that I am acquiring and serving, cell by cell. However, in this new cell I can preach the Gospel in peace for only three days. On the morning of the fourth day, I hear a suspicious fumbling at the cell door. The door unlocks with a creak. The official with the gold epaulettes enters once more, accompanied by a *korpusnoi*.

"There's singing in this cell every day!" he declares with official sternness. Silence.

"Who's singing?" the accompanying officer shouts, raising his voice.

"I am singing." I reply with studied cheer.

"Oh, you're singing? Why are you singing?"

"I am a Christian and I am in prison. The apostles Paul and Silas also sang in prison, to keep from falling into despair. And that is the reason I am singing too."

This man has not heard my story yet, and lets me finish what I have to say. He turns on his heel and leaves. Nobody takes down my name. My cellmates, who recognize him as the prison's program chief, tell me that he is a kindly man. The next morning, nobody comes in to bother me, and I dare to hope that he will let me continue my spiritual activities at my discretion. This cell has not finished learning the song. We spend the last evening learning it with special diligence.

That evening, the command of *otboi*[7]*!* ("Down for the night!") is issued through the *kormushk* as usual. I lie down on my bunk like a dutiful prisoner.

7 *otboi* – "Down for the night!": an order that all the men must be on the bunks

But that night, when I least expect it, I am awakened from a deep sleep: "Haamer, Harri Aleksandrovich, date of birth 1906."

"Yes," I reply through a curtain of sleep.

"Come along, with all your things!"

Yes, of course, they must be transferring me to yet another cell. But why in the middle of the night?

The *korpusnoi* leads the way and I follow. A fine man, I think; he trusts me not to push him.

The guard of the next corridor opens the iron bars of the gate and locks them behind us once again. We go through another set of gates, and we are there.

"Wait here," orders the *korpusnoi*, and disappears.

I wait. Suddenly, my eyes find the cell door where they have left me standing. The number on it is 17. My heart sinks. Are they really going to throw me into "India?" My fearful imagination has not yet been able to take full flight when the *korpusnoi* returns, opens the door to Cell 17, and seals my destiny with a single phrase - "Get in!" The lock creaks behind me, and my body and soul are left to the mercy of criminals that strike fear into the entire prison population.

A lamp burns in the ceiling. The men sleep on bunks, lying on their backs with their faces uncovered, according to prison rules. I can meet them all right there. In sleep, their faces are not so frightening. But one of them has propped himself up on his bunk and is questioning me in Russian: "Who are you?" "I am a human being," I tell him anxiously, to which he replies: "A genuine human being, with dick and all. I can see that. How many people have you wasted to be thrown in here?"

"Not one." I say in my defense, startled.

"You a smasher?" he inquires.

I do not know that vernacular for "burglar." However, I have a pretty good idea that it does not describe my field of activity and I reply "No."

"Then you're just a simple thief?"

It is terribly unfortunate that I have to answer this patient young man's last question in the negative as well. Hearing that, his neighbor, who has awakened, remarks, "He ain't one of us," and falls asleep once more.

I ask this sensible thief where I might lie down. He indicates a spot on the floor near the *parask*[8] (metal latrine bucket).

I spread out the blanket I have brought along from home, cover myself with my coat and try to sleep, leaving myself in God's grace.

After we are awakened, allowed to use the toilet and wash, the real interrogation begins. It is conducted by an old thief with a hardened face and a look in his eyes that was so frightening that it could convince anyone that this man might choke him to death.

However, when he hears that I am a pastor, he respectfully leaves me in peace. Nobody cares when one of the young punks insults me by saying "You - with the long hair and short wit" Nobody pays any attention to me. They have their own stories, their own plans, their own jokes. And I do not try to contribute to their conversations. Only God knows how long I can keep quietly to myself among them. I am dispirited, and my outlook less than rosy.

But then something happens.

Around midday, before we hear the racket of the meal-bucket being brought to our door, the *kormushk* is opened and my name is called. I am to come out and receive a package. I get up and go to the opening. I am already being shadowed by two "Indians." No sooner do I give my signature than they grab the parcel and dump its entire contents into a box. Of course, they plan to distribute the goods. Fifty percent of everything belongs to them.

I catch a glimpse of the sorry contents of the package; it has been hacked into small pieces. Ham and boiled potatoes, radishes and cookies, all reduced to a hideous mush. Apparently, this is how the prison administration is trying to keep me in line. I have little desire to stuff myself with this slop. Still, I make a stern face and tell the boys, "Get your hands off! This package is mine and I can do whatever I want with it."

The roomful of pickpockets is suddenly attentive. They had not expected a man of the cloth to act this way. Before they can intervene, I place the box containing the remnants of my package onto the table and declare, "This, my brothers, is all for you. In God's name, you may eat it." The men rise

8 *parask* – Latrine bucket; usually a barrel crudely cut in half

from their places. One that has risen to get his share argues, "No, only fifty percent of it is ours."

"No, not fifty percent. I want to give it all to you and I will do so. The prison swill is enough for me."

"Well, *batyushka*[9], if that's how you feel, you can at least come and share with us," declares the old recidivist, who seems to be the chief in here, in a friendly tone.

I sit at the table with the thieves, bless myself and my handful of food with the sign of the cross, and eat.

That is how I formed a bond of brotherhood with those fellows, the ones that the prison administration had deemed to be the most suitable companions for me.

The most memorable days of my life in prison began right here.

They wanted me to sit with them and tell them a story. I talked and talked. I told them of sin, and the awakening of conscience, and the grace of God, and redemption through the sacrificial blood of Jesus Christ. They listened. The entire cell listened from morning until night. The cell's "cow"[10]listened too. The "cow" was occasionally taken out to be "milked," after which he returned and sat with us again. And so I lived in "India" for nearly a month, until my trial. Nobody fought me for any of the other packages I received. Arkadi, the young Russian in the military shirt who slept in the next bunk, said to me: "Father, if we end up in the same camp, and somebody there insults you, I'll stab him to death." I did not doubt that he would do so, because he had plenty of experience, having killed three people already.

When I was taken to trial, they all shook my hand in farewell. The Chief kissed me three times. And I blessed him.

---

9 *Batyushka* – Father, bishop, Patriarch; common usage for Orthodox clergy

10 *"cow" to be "milked"* – A prisoner placed into each cell as a snitch; the authorities would periodically remove him from the cell so that he could tell them about what was being said and done there

TELL US ABOUT YOUR CRIMES

I was only interrogated at night, as if the process fears the light of day. Those poor interrogators. I was depriving them of their night's rest.

My first interrogator is named Major Zaitsev. Of course, it is possible that each of these security men have several different names.

He is a very polite middle-aged officer who takes his job very seriously.

The guard takes me from Cell 13 of the Pagari Street building through several corridors and up some narrow stairways to a large room, where he hands me over to a man with golden epaulettes who introduces himself as Major Zaitsev. There is no need for me to introduce myself, since my file lays on the table in front of him.

Still, he has to record all the formalities into my interrogation record. I must answer his questions about my surname, given name, patronymic[11] and date of birth.

After he has recorded the answers to those questions, he turns to me and begins amicably, "All right, now please tell me about your crimes."

"Crimes?" I ask, astonished.

"Indeed, please tell me truthfully: why have you been arrested and why are the Soviet authorities forced to punish you?"

"Excuse me, but I have no idea why I've been arrested or what crimes I have committed, to force the Soviet authorities to punish me," I insist stubbornly.

---

11 *patronymic* – Middle name; shows father's name; "Mikailovich," son of Mikail

"Think about it carefully," the polite *chekist* says. He lights a cigarette and leaves the room.

He lets me sit alone and wait for quite some time. When he returns, I am dozing. And since I am unable to come up with a satisfactory response, he sends me back down to the cellar. Undoubtedly, he has failed to fulfill his plan for that night. But perhaps he has had more success with his interrogations of other "criminals."

I sit in the basement cell for a week or more and ponder whatever crimes I may have committed. I can think of a few deeds that are deserving of God's wrath, but nothing that would require me to appear before a Soviet court. I have not fought in any army, nor taken part in any conspiracy. I have never slandered Soviet authorities nor praised the shameful actions of the Fascists. Instead, I have saved communists from death camps, sheltered members of underground movements, published an underground religious youth magazine during the German occupation, given sermons opposing the persecution of Jews. Truly, I do not have the slightest inkling why the Soviet courts would want to punish me.

The more I puzzle over it, the more incomprehensible the motives for my arrest become. Finally, I escape the mental nightmare by puzzling no longer. My attention is consumed by the physical living conditions in this basement, which are unbearable. The men sit on the floor, naked. The sweat pours down our sides incessantly. The ventilation system is perpetually out of order. We have developed a system of taking turns: each man is given some time to breathe fresh air coming from a crack, a few centimeters wide, between the door and the floor. This "fresh air" carries the scent of the musty corridor, but compared to the stuffy dampness of our cell, it is still fresh air. In the dank air of our cell, the chunk of bread we get each morning is moldy by the evening.

When my wife brings me a package, we have to eat its contents immediately. We cannot save a single mouthful for the next day. Of course, the thirteen of us in that cell can devour the food in no time at all.

We are allowed to speak only in whispers. If anyone dares to raise his voice, the guard will hiss through the hatch: "Quiet!"

And still, I can preach the Gospel to my cellmates, even if I must whisper. In whispers, we share our life stories. In whispers, we discuss our outlook for the future. In whispers, we even argue.

Our only change of scenery is the daily fifteen-minute walk in the prison's narrow yard, where we must follow each other in single file, our hands behind our back. No one is allowed to say a word or to look up. But no one says we cannot to fill our lungs with the cool, fresh winter air.

But after this respite in the fresh air, it is even harder to return to the stale, hot and humid cell.

When I have finished telling my stories, I sit there staring at the crushed remnants of a louse, trying to ascertain how much it has dried since yesterday.

I starti to think they have forgotten all about me when they come one night and take me to another interrogation.

Major Zaitsev has apparently kept the previous interrogation record, and can skip the questions about my first and last name, patronymic and date of birth. He gets right down to business.

"So, have you given some thought to your criminal activity?"

"Yes, I'm so terribly sorry I was so unfair to my son. He was sick in bed when I was taken away, and I thought he was being lazy. I have been stern with him all too often, and impatient when I thought he was not studying diligently enough. That is the greatest crime that has come to mind. I truly wish I could make amends."

The investigator calmly lets me finish my statement. Then he fixes me with a harsh stare and silently summons the guard. The interrogation is over.

"That was quick!" grunts the guard as he shoves me into the cell.

That night, sleep does not come. I wonder what they will do to me now?

But each day passes like the one before. Twice a day, we are fed. Twice a day, we are counted. We are also taken to the bathhouse with bullet holes in the walls. The men know that people were killed here in 1941. One of the chief executioners, a *korpusnoi*, earned the rank of second lieutenant. For some reason, that stocky officer with the pockmarked face was nicknamed King Kong. Without a doubt, anyone meeting a face like his in the dark would stop in his tracks. During the head counts, he does not behave like a brute, although his eyes betray what he might be capable of.

Two weeks pass and I am not called. Perhaps they have forgotten me. I receive no more packages. Perhaps the investigator is punishing me for not "honestly" confessing my crimes. The men in my cell think that I will be sent home soon. My heart becomes heavier, the longer I am left in peace. Still, I pick my brain, trying to recall anything that the Soviet authorities could punish me for, anything at all. If they interrogate me again, I will not deny it.

Scurvy begins to gnaw at my body. My feet swell, and festering sores appear on them. Some days I am so exhausted that I hardly feel like going out for my walk. Still, I force myself to eat and dress for the walk.

Suddenly, I am summoned in the middle of the day. "That's a good sign," my cellmates assure me.

The same interrogation room, this time with two officers. My old "friend" has enlisted the help of a heavyset captain. It seems that I am a tough nut to crack.

Now the captain is questioning me. They both have sheets of paper for taking notes. When I have introduced myself with my first and last name and patronymic, the captain asks, "Tell me, why did you stay here in Estonia?"

"To serve my people," I reply.

"Hah! To serve your people. You didn't stay here to serve your people, but to betray them. And now the people will judge you!" he snarls angrily.

"What do you mean, judge me? I haven't met a single member of my nationality here. I am forced to speak Russian with you, and even the guard standing outside is a foreigner. Please tell me, where are my people, the ones who are to judge me?" I ask, protesting.

"Fine. You want to meet a member of your nationality here. We have a few." Having said that, the fierce captain gets up and leaves the room. The major is silent, doodling on his paper. A short time later, the captain returns with a hunchbacked Jew. Without introducing himself, the newcomer asks, with a marked roll to his r's: "What is your name?" "Haamer," I reply. "Haamer, yes, Haamer, and what is your profession?" asks my "compatriot."

"I am a pastor."

"Pastor, yes, a pastor. How long have you worked as a pastor?" asks the Hebrew.

"Twenty years."

"Twenty years. That's a long time. They've let you wear your black coat for too long. It's about time we stripped it off your back!" snarls the Jew on behalf of my people, and leaves.

I turn to the officer, who has understood not one word of our exchange, and say, "Thank you for proving your claim. The proof was more than satisfactory."

"Now, you see," says the major calmly, "you can tell me about your crimes."

"Yes, now I can tell you what you're interested in hearing," I say meaningfully.

Both interrogators prepare to take notes.

"I am a thief," I say to their astonishment. They stare at me for a moment, eyes wide with surprise. Then the captain says, "You're a thief. Are you stealing bread from your comrades in the cell?"

"No, not that. But I steal something every day by glancing up at the blue heaven above."

"What do you mean?" asks the major curiously.

"Every day, when we are taken for our walk, I steal a glance at the blue heaven above."

"Why do you steal that?" the captain inquires.

"Because it is forbidden."

"Who forbids it?" the captain barks in sudden aggravation, coming over to stand directly in front of me.

"The sadists you have assigned to guard us," I reply calmly.

He strikes me on the head. Sparks dance before my eyes. Protecting my face with my hands, I wait for the next blow, but it never comes. The captain returns to his seat, hissing with rage. I tell him, with all the bitterness of a degraded prisoner: "And even if you poke out my eyes, you can never keep me from looking to the heavens."

They exhange a few quiet words. The captain leaves the room, never giving me another glance, and does not return. I never see him again in my life.

The major discovers a file and finds something in it to read. After looking it over, he starts asking me about people who have tried to escape across the border. Do I know any such people? Yes, I remember that incident with the provocateur.

I tell him how a small man secretly entered my chancellery one day and asked to speak to me privately. He introduced himself as Adossor. The major begins to write diligently. I describe the event in vivid detail, telling him how the man said he had heard I was a kindly person who was helping people escape across the bay to Finland. I asked the provocateur where he had heard about this. "At the women's clinic," replied the dimwit. I escorted that man to the door, suggesting that he go and dig up some more foolish gossip, because the clinic was a place where lots of women congregated and gossip was rampant.

"But why didn't you report this man to the authorities?" asks the interrogator with feigned sternness.

"I didn't have to, because you were the ones who sent him in the first place." He does not mention the incident any more.

"But haven't you attempted to conceal any criminals from the Soviet authorities?" asks the major, changing the subject.

"How could I have concealed any criminals?"

"Well, by issuing them some false documents and helping them get passports."

"As far as false documents, it's possible that I've issued thousands. All our congregation's records were destroyed when our church burned down on August 25, 1944. When I tried to reconstruct the records, people would come to help me out, giving me the information verbally. Whenever anyone needed a document issued on the basis of church records, I did so without further inquiry. I did realize that Soviet law regards any document issued by a pastor on the basis of congregation records to be just a piece of paper, and not an official document. If you want to prosecute anyone for illegal activity, you'll have to arrest the police authorities who issued passports on the basis of those church documents. It is not my responsibility to check the identities of each person that gave me his or her name, especially since our congregation registers contained nearly 20,000 names at the time." My explanation seems to satisfy him.

He has nothing more to ask me, neither does he require my signature on the interrogation records.

Apparently, my case is a confusing one.

Even now, it seems that the investigators are still lacking the justification they need to hand me over to the "harsh but fair" Soviet justice system. Soon thereafter, I am returned to the cell.

I have wasted enough of his time, and his plan is still unfulfilled.

In my heart, I know that my case is not over yet. Otherwise, the Deputy for Religious Affairs would not have said, "We'll have to discipline you in some other way." This deputy had also been a member of the security apparatus.

I am sure they will find something for which to sentence me to a dozen years or so.

(This story is from the basement of the KGB[12] building on Pagari Street, February 1948.)

12 *KGB* – Soviet secret police; spies and enforcers of the Communist state

HOPELESSNESS HAS NO PLACE IN OUR PROGRAM

Every ten days they take us to the bathhouse, which is located in the basement of Patarei Prison. We get there by passing through drafty, dismal passages. Word has it that people had been killed there. They were killed by the Russians, and then the Germans, and then again by the Russians.

It is ultimately irrelevant whether these people were killed there or somewhere else. But there is lots of writing on the walls and benches of the bath. Names, dates, sentences. It is like a mailbox through which friends and perfect strangers inform each other of their fate. So many names are followed by a date and the note: "sentenced to death." On the lid of a nightstand in Cell 8 of the quarantine wing, I found the last words of the first person sentenced to death. His name was Voldemar Tammaru, sentenced to death on December 24, 1945. He was shoved into that cell on Christmas Eve to await execution by shooting. Perhaps on that same Christmas Eve night, an executioner in red epaulettes put a bullet into the back of his head in that bathhouse corridor. I can never make the walk down that horrible passage to the baths with a peaceful heart. And yet, the bath is nothing but a ceiling with showerheads. The ones that happen to be working dribble enough warm water onto you to let you rinse off all the soap. Of course, there is also an oven for roasting clothing, called "hell for lice," and a barber. The only shaving apparatus that the barber knows how to use are hair clippers. This means that we, the prisoners, are never smoothly shaven. However, anybody who wants to have his chin scraped shiny smooth can have it done in the cell, using a shard of glass. Some fellows are adept at finding and concealing shards of glass, experts who can give you a smoother shave with a piece of glass than with the finest Swedish blade. But I never feel the urge to have it done. Why irritate your skin by scraping at it over and over again?

The prisoners from the hospital wing bathe according to the same procedures as the prisoners from the general cells, with one exception. The residents of any two cells from the hospital wing are allowed to bathe together.

One day, Cells 4 and 5 of the hospital wing happen to be washing together in the bathhouse. I see a horribly thin stranger sitting on the bench, his face so sad that I cannot help but feel sorry for him. No one talks to him. His eyes are fixed in a glassy stare on the filthy bathhouse floor, and neither hand picks up the soap to lather his body. The man looks so typically German that I begin speaking to him in German.

It turns out that he is indeed a German soldier, imprisoned for the second time. He had been caught stealing salt from a warehouse where he had been working, carrying sacks of salt. He had stuffed a few handfuls of salt into his pocket. Now, he was awaiting the "harsh but fair" sentence of a Soviet court for committing this crime.

As he tells me his story, he becomes even more dejected. Somehow, I want to console this man from a foreign land. I ask if he is a Christian. He replies "yes."

"But as Christians, we must know that hopelessness has no place in our program," I tell him.

"How can that be?" the German protests. "Our outlook is so hopeless. Death will be my only escape!" the miserable man cries.

"Do you know the story of Jesus and his disciple on the stormy Lake Genetsareth?" I ask him.

"Of course I do," he replies.

"Then you know what he said to his fearful friends when they cried: 'Teacher, rise! We are doomed!'"

"He asked them: 'Where is your faith?'"

"Yes, he asked them that," I affirm. "And do you know why he asked them that?"

The German becomes thoughtful.

"He had a reason for asking them that question. In their fear of death, they had lost their faith in their teacher. They saw nothing else but the storm, and they were frightened by the waves crashing over the boat. But they did not know Jesus well enough to have enough faith to follow Him, even into death. To go with Him into death is not the same as to perish. If they had drowned in the lake along with Jesus, they would not have perished.

There is no situation into which we cannot go with Christ. If we have faith in Him, we will not perish, even if we should die. And that is why hopelessness has no place in our program."

The German listens to me attentively.

"Do you understand?" I ask.

"I understand very well. I have never appreciated my Christian faith from that perspective. But it would truly be wonderful if I could feel that way. Then, there would be no more hopelessness in our lives. Not in any situation. No, that would be unspeakably wonderful."

And the sad man's eyes show a trace of a glimmer.

"You have comforted me so well. What may I do for you in return?" the thin man asks, brightening.

"You may wash my back," I reply. And he starts scrubbing my back so energetically that I soon have to stop him, fearing that he will rub it raw. Of course, I scrub his back as well.

And so we form a union whose slogan is: "Hopelessness has no place in our program!"

A few days later, I get the Russian thief, that young girl who cleans the hospital rooms, to take him a small gift. He sends a reply written with a pencil stub on the margin of a scrap of paper torn from a newspaper. In addition to brief thanks, the missive contains the underlined words: *"In unserem Programm gibts keine Hoffnungslosigkeit."*

(This recollection is from Patarei Hospital, April 1948.)

MY NAME IS DEARLY BELOVED

That limping three-striper[13] known for his excessive zeal was nicknamed "The Skier." He was one of the most vile guards ever to sit in the "dovecote" of the guard turret and watch over prisoners as we spent the twenty minutes of our exercise period walking in the yard by Patarei Prison.

Because the political prisoners would stubbornly try to communicate with each other in the yards during the exercise period, they no longer allowed the denizens of political prisoners' cells to exercise in neighboring yards at the same time.

But I am a resident of "India," and Cell 11, which is populated by political prisoners, is allowed to exercise in the yard next to ours.

Lyonka is the son of a colonel. However, thanks to all the robberies and murders he has committed, he is probably more famous than his military father. He wastes no time in hooking up with others of his ilk from the political prisoners' cells. Soon, he is communicating with a "comrade" in the next yard through a chink in the wall. I am reasonably sure that my colleague Dean Lääne, a pastor from Märjamaa, is being held in that cell. I ask Lyonka to get Lääne to the chink in the wall. But The Skier has snapped to attention. He shouts at Lyonka, who ignores him. Before I can count to three, Lyonka whispers to me, "Lääne is at the fence," and immediately turns to curse at The Skier in the foulest language. That is my signal to start talking with my colleague.

---

13 *three-striper* – Arm-patch of a sergeant; more advanced rank in the Soviet army

“Hello, brother. Best greetings on this cherished Sunday. May the grace and peace of the Father of Light be with you.”

“Hello, prophet of Paul. How are you?” says Lääne, trying to sound cheerful.

“All right, just like you. Who will be in your pulpit today?”

I cannot ask him any more. The Skier is already barking at me from his dovecote, threatening me with several days of punishment in the cold cell.

He threatens Lyonka with the same. But he has not noticed Lääne.

My positive mood vanishes immediately, because the things I have heard about the cold cell are less than pleasant. I have no doubt that The Skier will make good on his threat, because there is not a shadow of mercy in his monstrous face.

Forlornly, I go over to Lyonka and express my regret for dragging him into this situation.

But that nineteen-year-old miscreant is wiser and more experienced than I, and he reassures me by saying: “Father, don’t worry. Do everything I do, and everything will be fine.”

Our twenty minutes of breathing fresh air are over. From his perch above us, The Skier hands us over to the female corridor guard, who will take us back to our cell. Pointing at Lyonka and me, he declares that both of us will be sent to the black hole.

The fair-haired maiden gestures for us to follow her and takes us to the cell door. There, she begins to take roll. When it is Lyonka’s turn, she stops and begins making notes into a notebook. She asks the boy: “Surname?”

Lyonka replies: “Sidorov.”

“Given name?”

“Vyacheslav,” he lies, without batting an eye.

“Father’s name?”

“Ivan.” End of conversation. Lyonka slips into the cell.

I am the last in line. When it is my turn, the procedure is repeated: “Surname?” the epauletted maiden asks.

I reply: “Beloved.” She dutifully records this in her notebook.

“Given name?”

“Dearly.” Lyonka has taught me well.

“Father’s name?”

"August."

Everything is duly noted. For good measure, she also asks me: "Date of birth?"

She had not asked Lyonka for his date of birth. But I am sure I must lie in response to this question as well.

"1911." I am delighted to make myself five years younger, although most certainly I could or would not make any advances on this Russian girl.

I enter the cell with more dignity than Lyonka. I actually bow to the guard. In all my other actions, I imitated everything my wise advisor had done.

Not until the following evening do they begin looking for Sidorov and Beloved in the cells. They start with Cell 17. The *korpusnoi* shouts through the *kormushka*: "Sidorov!" No response. He calls again and again, until someone grunts, "He was transferred to another cell!" The *korpusnoi* is satisfied. Then he calls out the other name: "Beloved!" Lyonka shouts back: "He was taken away on a prisoner transport!"

The hatch snaps shut and we are left in peace.

Later, when I was at Lasnamäe Prison, waiting to be taken away on that first prisoner transport, my Baptist colleague Kallis (*"Beloved"*) told me that they had threatened him with the cold cell one day for no apparent reason. They had double-checked his personal information, and the evident discrepancies had confused them. Although the surname was the same, his given names and date of birth were not the ones they were looking for. He was returned to his regular cell.

I have no idea how long they continued to search for Vyacheslav Sidorov and Dearly Beloved in that prison.

(This happened in May 1948 at Patarei Prison.)

MY BREAD IS THROWN IN THE TRASH

I have never been a believer in dreams. However, every morning after they wake us, my cellmates ask me to interpret their dreams. Each man believes he has dreamt something meaningful. And woe to me if I should interpret any of these visions as predicting something bad for the future.

In Lasnamäe Prison, before my long journey on the prisoner transport, I myself have an unusual dream. At the prison, the words "transport, transport" echo in our ears; we wait and prepare. None of us dare to hope that we can escape being taken away on this transport. In the life of a prisoner, those two weeks in anticipation of the transport are the most anguishing of all. The men are quiet and depressed. They cannot even curse the lice swarming over the cots in our cell. We try to sing together. I try to comfort them with the eternal Gospel, but in their dejection and anguish, they are comforted by nothing. Whenever they do speak, it is of the Siberian camps. Some have heard that conditions at the camps are better than those at Vasalemma or Mustamäe, but others speak of them as hell, where people are skinned alive, where their nails are yanked out.

That final night in the Lasnamäe holding cell, I have a dream about the fate that will befall me on the following day. The dream goes like this. From an endless line of men, they select me and a young man whose face I do not recognize. Once this army of men has gone, the two of us look around in the empty prison cells. The young man suddenly disappears from my side, and an officer appears, silently beckoning me to follow him. I obey the officer's order, following him down a spiral staircase, farther and farther down. Finally, we reach a large group of men that he beckons me to join, whereupon he disappears. After that, the dream becomes hazy.

I have no idea how to interpret this dream. However, its meaning becomes clear enough on the following morning.

The prison corridor is bustling with activity. Cell doors are being opened, the rumble of footsteps echoes and then fades in the corridor. All the men in my cell are quiet as mice. When will it be our turn? We look through the barred window. People are standing on the street below. A young soldier arrested in Kronstadt with three Estonian boys and sentenced to ten years for criticizing the Army's miserable grub recognizes his mother and sister among the people standing outside. Perhaps they have heard about the transports being prepared, perhaps they came in from Märjamaa in the hopes of seeing their son and brother once more. He sees them, but they do not know where to look to find him. If we shout, can they hear us?

"Jürisalu, let's sing! Maybe they'll notice us then!" And we sing, and are soon joined by the entire cell. Nobody comes to quiet us. The people on the street start looking up in our direction. Jürisalu presses his nose against the window, staring and singing. Suddenly, a broad smile lights up his face. "They're waving, they're waving! They recognized me!" He is happy. They are truly waving, as are others. The people looking in our direction wipe their eyes and wave until the police arrive to drive them away.

My eyes also seek one special person, but she is waiting to see me for one last time at another location.

Then it is our cell's turn. The lock and bolt clang simultaneously, and forty men must respond "*yest*[14]*!*" in turn, as each one's name is called.

My name is the only one not called. I begin to feel a bit uneasy.

The other men are sent into the corridor after roll call. The *korpusnoi* orders me to stay in the cell.

The thunder of footsteps. The men of my cell are taken away.

Then, a two-striper[15] arrives and takes me to another cell. A young man is standing by the window. As I greet him, he seems somehow familiar. He

14 *yest* – "I'm here"

15 *two-striper* – Arm patch of a mid-ranking officer in the Soviet army

explains that he has been left behind by the transport because he has a hernia. That must mean that I, too, have been left behind. I feel the weight lifting from my heart. Soon, the same two-striper returns and takes me to a cell at the end of the corridor. It contains lots of men. I realize that we have been placed in the sick prisoners' cell. They have all been left behind by the prisoner transports. One man approaches me as if he knows me. He greets me and introduces himself as the Baptist preacher Kallis. He makes room for me on his bunk, where we discuss our fate. Suddenly, I recall the incident in Patarei Prison's Cell 17, when I escaped punishment in the black hole by claiming my name was Dearly Beloved (*"Armas Kallis"*). I ask if he had ever been threatened with the black hole during his time in Patarei. He tells me how he had unexpectedly been taken to the door of the cold cell one evening. However, once they realized that his name, date of birth, and other statistics did not correspond with those of the prisoner they were looking for, they sent him back to his cell. Now, after finally learning the reason behind that incident, he finds it rather amusing. I look around the cell, trying to discern opportunities for spreading the Gospel. The door opens suddenly and an officer steps in. His appearance takes me aback. Although I have never seen him before in my life, he also seems familiar, just like the young man with the hernia. It is then that I remember my dream. Nobody has to tell me that the officer has come for me.

He holds a sheet of paper, from which he reads a single name: "Haamer?"

"*Yest.*"

"Given name and patronymic?"

"Harri, son of Aleksander."

"Date of birth?"

"1906."

"Prepare yourself and your belongings."

I grab my coat, blanket and bundle from the bunk. I call "Good bye, brothers!" and leave. And then the officer leads me down a spiral staircase. Exactly like in the dream.

Apparently, they are missing one from the total number of prisoners to be transported. And the lot falls to me. Now the person compiling the list of transportees can sleep well: he has fulfilled his plan.

There are no men anywhere in sight. The yard is littered with papers, letters, books, bowls and pots confiscated during the search. They are just finishing the search of the women. I find out that the women will be transported along with us. It seems that, with the exception of the sick prisoners' cell, Lasnamäe Prison has been emptied completely.

The officer hands me over to a soldier, who orders me to take off my clothes right there. The all-too-familiar thievery begins once again. And yet, the only loot that this man with the red epaulettes gets from me is my wife's letter, my belt and my New Testament. He orders me to read the letter and throw it away. That is how I must say good-bye to my wife, tearing to pieces the letter that I have kept with me as kind of a talisman. He puts my belt aside and throws the New Testament into a garbage bin.

I turn to the soldier with a question that startles him: "Why did you throw my bread into the trash bin?"

"What do you mean – your bread?"

"Look, that book is my bread. If I cannot read it, I will starve to death."

The Russian boy's interest is aroused. He retrieves my New Testament from the trash bin and asks: "What kind of book is this?"

"It is God's Word."

"Then it's a Bible?" he asks. "But you're not allowed to take it with you."

"But if I ask you for permission, is it still not allowed?"

Apparently, this soldier has his heart in the right place. He stops a passing officer and shows him my book. The officer says, "All right, give it to him," but is suddenly seized by doubts, and takes my treasure to a table where several other officers sit. In the meantime, I have dressed myself once again and approach the table to sign for the things that have been taken from me.

My belt and my New Testament lie on the table. Neither one is returned to me. My belt is confiscated because I could use it to hang myself. My New Testament is kept from me because I might use it to spread propaganda.

A haughty captain sitting at the table reassures me: "You'll get it back when we get there."

"But I'm asking you to give it to me now. We may have a very long trip. And if I cannot read this book, I will die," I beg.

"Then write your name in the book. That way I'll know it's yours and you'll get it back when we get there," the captain replies stubbornly.

Once again, I turn to him beseechingly. "Please let me take the book with me. If you don't let me keep my book, you might as well not give me any bread at all."

"Go," says the captain darkly.

I leave them very sadly. I turn around to look at them one more time. He calls me back, takes my book from the table and gives it to me, grunting: "Take your book."

I thank him and bless him to the best of my ability. Then, they open the door of a cell filled with men, some who I know, some who are strangers.

The men shower me with questions, utterly amazed that I would be registered for the long prisoner transport. They had all been convinced that I would be spared.

I then tell them about my dream, the one that came true so soon and so precisely. I share my provisions with them, the ones which my wife managed to give me at the last minute. They now seem excessive, and I have nowhere to keep them anyway. Finally, I show them my most valuable loaf of bread, which the grace of God has saved from the garbage bin.

My book would have met the same fate as my belt, which I never saw again, even though I had given them my signature.

But this world is teeming with foolishness and lies.

(Lasnamäe Prison, July 19, 1948.)

WHY DID YOU HIT ME?

It is our third day of travel. Calculating the number of rail cars, I conclude that this is an enormous transport train, with 400 to 500 cars. Nobody has any idea where we are being taken.

Thirty-two silent men sit slumped on their bunks. There is little conversation.

Someone in the car has a pencil nub. Somewhere they manage to find some paper, and we write our final greetings to those we leave behind. I tear off a scrap of paper that my frisker overlooked in my coat pocket, and write my last words to my wife and children: "I face my unknown fate with the knowledge that good things come to those who love God." I add my wife's address to the tiny missive, and a note asking the person who finds it to send it to my wife.

Between Tapa and Kadrina, I throw the missive out through a crack in the floor of the train car. A rail worker found my final message on the railway embankment and actually sent it to my wife. Many thanks to him, whoever he may be.

Naturally, our rail car also carries an informer. I must throw my letter out of the rail car without anyone noticing. We all have to be careful about what we say; we must behave in a way that will guarantee no additional unpleasant surprises at the end of our journey.

The first day, I read my New Testament only to the SS-officer[16] lying beside me. Later, I become more bold.

---

16 *SS officer* – Special police unit in Hitler's army

Through the barred windows of the cattle car, the golden meadows and green forests of my homeland wave their last good-bye. For three days now, the engine has been puffing through the Russian scrub, through villages and towns scorched by war. We stop at a station near Leningrad.

A search is conducted at almost every stop. This entails first knocking on the car door with a large hammer. Once this is done, a *konvoi*[17] enters to do a head count. Two soldiers, one two-striper and one three-striper, assist him by serving as "tamers." The three-striper is a Russian kid with a crude, ugly face. He attacks us like a tiger.

There is an empty space between the two doors. Bunks are located at either end of our rail car. During the head count, we must assemble at one end of the car, and as soon as they begin counting, each counted person mush dash to the other end of the car as quickly as possible. Whether he ends up running into a bunk or sliding under a bunk is his own problem. The head count is conducted like this: "First!" and the nearest man gets whacked on his back with the hammer. "Second! third!..." Nobody escapes being hit on the back with the hammer. Thirty-two times the three-striper shouts his numbers, and thirty-two times he raises the hammer for a blow at the back of each prisoner.

On the first day, we endure the blows in silence. On the second day, dissent begins to grow. I say: "We must resist. They are not allowed to hit us like that."

But the men are wiser, saying: "There is no way that we can resist. You'll just be given a longer sentence if you do."

And so we ride on. The *konvois* (convoy guards) sit in their dovecotes at each end of the car, calling us "f---ing fascists." The man with red epaulettes enters the car to whack us with the hammer once again. What a wonderful outlook for the rest of our sentence!

On the third day, I decide to resist, despite warnings from my fellow sufferers.

It happens at the stop after Leningrad.

Again, a search. Again, the sadistic Communist Youth three-striper is in his element. "First!" - smack against the scruff, "Second!" – another whack.

17 *konvoi* – Convoy guard

I am the seventh in line to receive the blow. But he does not raise his hand to strike the next man.

"Why did you hit me?" I shout at the brat, looking him straight in the eye.

"I shouldn't just hit you, I should kill you, you f---ing fascist," he hisses.

But I dart to the door of the rail car and begin pounding on it with my fists.

"What are you doing?" the *konvoi* shrieks, livid with rage.

"I am summoning the commander of this train," I reply and continue my pounding. All the men in my rail car have turned deathly pale. We do not have to wait long; we hear the yelping of the dogs and rapid footsteps approaching our rail car.

"Open it!" they shout from outside.

The two-striper opens the car doors. In climbs the captain I met in the yard at Lasnamäe. Soldiers, their automatic rifles cocked, stay outside, waiting in anticipation.

"What's going on here?" the captain asks, more than a little irritated.

"I am being beaten!"

"Who is beating you?"

"That three-striper."

If that thug had been able to pass sentence on me at that moment, I am sure he would have killed me. I could see it in his face.

"What did he hit you with?"

"That stick he is holding."

"Did he hit anyone else?"

Silence. Had he not also hit that SS-officer? I am amazed at the kind of company I am keeping in my car.

However, the captain seems to understand full well what has been going on. He does not order them to remove me from the car or shackle me. He looks over at the three-striper and turns toward the prisoners, saying calmly:

"This will be investigated."

He also asks: "Are there any other complaints?" Silence. But I am encouraged by the captain's calm demeanor and continue: "That *konvoi* at the end of the car keeps insulting us by saying 'f---ing nation.' We are a very unfortunate nation, and we do not deserve that kind of insulting language."

He listens calmly to my complaint and says: "No, nobody should be allowed to insult your nationality." He leaves, trailed by the armed soldiers and the dogs.

At the next stop, the three-striper comes to the head count without his club. Each time, he recognizes me, and each time, he promises to kill me. Apparently, this boy can hold a grudge. But he never again raises his hand to strike the prisoners. Apparently he has learned a bit of a lesson.

Whe are taken off the train for a bathing stop in Omsk. As we approach the bathhouse, I see that *konvoi* holding a gun. But my fellow prisoners keep me in the middle of the crowd, protecting me from being shot, which certainly would have happened if I had been at the end of the line, or if I had happened to stumble or accidentally take a false step.

After I wash myself, the colleague of that three-striper brute, the two-striper in charge of our rail car, comes and sits down next to me. He starts talking to me. He asks:

"*Batja*[18], who were you as a free man?"

"A clergyman."

"Imagine that! You're a good fellow after all," he says, and then rises to line up the prisoners.

(Summer, 22. July 1948.)

---

18 *Batja* – "Father," a term Russians used for all clergy; perhaps said in derision

...WHERE MY SOUL CAN BREATHE SO FREE

Novosibirsk station. An old Estonian from Siberia recognizes the approach.

Naturally, we are not taken to the grand station entrance of Siberia's largest metropolis. Our train stops on auxiliary tracks some distance away. In front of us, there are two other trains made up of cattle cars just like ours. They have the same barred windows and dovecotes on the roof. It means that others like us have been brought here too. Shortly after our train arrives, another train creeps onto another auxiliary track near us. The soldiers open the doors, and women and children emerge. Apparently, it is another trainload of deportees. Before we can satisfy our curiosity about that train, yet another train of cattle cars rolls up right beside us, bearing its human cargo. One of their window slits lines up with one of ours. We call out: "Brothers, where are you from?"

"Ukraine," reply the bearded faces.

But the red-epauletted[19] *komsomols*[20] are already coming over to stop our conversation.

Five trainloads of prisoners, all next to each other!

It must be an amazing sight. These trains carry at least two and a half thousand persons who have lost their freedom. They carry the pain and tears of two and a half thousand shattered families.

---

19 *red-epaulette* – Shoulder fringes on Communist Youth uniforms; this signified a lower rank

20 *Komsomol* – Young Communist League; membership was required of all young people

The trains will stop here for a few hours and quickly transport their cargo of fettered human beings to a place where they can be unloaded and shackled into slavery.

The station's loudspeakers are playing music.

"Listen!" I am nudged by my fellow traveler, a melancholy journalist whose pen will be left to gather dust for 25 years.

I listen. The loudspeakers are playing choral music. My ear catches a familiar melody with the lyrics: "I cannot find another land on earth where my soul can breathe so free."

Oh, what a mockery! Not for us, but for the governing powers who are using this song to proclaim how their people breathe free.

"Five trainloads of prisoners, and this is the song that echoes over them," the journalist says agitatedly.

"This would really be something to write about," I jibe sarcastically.

"Yes, what an article I'd have...and the Americans would pay in gold dollars for every line of it," he sighs, mourning his pen.

"And by the time it gets published, you'll be six feet under," I tell him, deflating his enthusiasm.

We stand there all day.

Our journey resumes at night. I wonder if they played the same record for the next trainload of prisoners.

I doubt that you could find another land such as this one on the face of our planet.

(Novosibirsk Station, late July, 1948.)

FLOWERS FROM THE VIADUCT

Once, while perusing a map of Siberia, I had found that Irkutsk lay rather close to Lake Baikal.

And now we have arrived in Irkutsk.

There may have been plenty of fine sights to see on this long journey. But as soon as anyone's face was seen nearing a window, the guard posted at one end of the car would start to swear. If that had no effect, he would toss pieces of coal at the window, threatening to shoot.

And yet, we saw several remarkable things.

Almost every rural station was surrounded by a settlement. Most of them included huts made of sod. These sod huts differed from each other only by the fact that some had a goat nibbling burdock leaves on the roof, whereas the roofs of other huts boasted a pig rooting in the sod.

Behind most stations ran a road, which was actually more like a wide, rutted path perhaps twenty meters wide. On these roads, we would occasionally see unusual draft animals – cows. Some cows were pulling empty wagons, some cows were harnessed to a load of hay. Each cow would walk slowly, udders swinging, with its mistress sitting in the wagon or lying sprawled on the hay, chewing a piece of straw.

We did not see any combines at work, although it was the season for harvesting rye. In some places, they were mowing with enormous hand-held sickles. I had never seen sickles like that before, although I had watched the harvesting of rye as a boy.

Village festivals were being held at some of the small stations where we stopped in the evenings. We heard accordions playing and girls singing. Behind one station, a village swing had been erected on the festival square.

But we are not allowed to look, because we are not tourists, but travelers on our way to a labor camp.

Now we have arrived in Irkutsk. Our train stops under a large viaduct. Vehicles and pedestrians pass over it.

A little girl leans over the viaduct's balustrade above us and looks down. Her face is so serious. She is too far away; I cannot tell whether she has blue eyes like my daughter's. And yet, she is there, almost like a manifestation of my own dear little daughter.

Undoubtedly, she knows what kind of train has stopped beneath her. Perhaps her own father had been taken far away from her on this kind of train. She cannot stop looking. People rush to and fro behind her, but she stands still and stares at our train.

Suddenly, the little girl turns away and vanishes.

We stop beneath that viaduct for several hours. The day is warm and the men are dozing on their bunks. However, the child has made me uneasy. Once again, my thoughts take me back across thousands of kilometers to the place from which I have been taken. My wife, my children, my home, my congregation, my friends – they all become so real that I want to cry out loud. I try to recall the details of the last things I did with my children, and the more I think about them, the more dejected I become.

I may have sat there by the window lost in my sorrow for several hours.

Suddenly, I notice something falling past the window. I look up. The little girl has returned and is scattering flowers onto the roof of our rail car.

No, I am not dreaming. She is standing there, her fair hair combed straight, wearing a light, colorful cotton dress, her feet probably bare. Her arms are brimming with white flowers, and she is scattering them down to us, the strangers below, behind the barred windows of their rail car.

Perhaps this is how she said farewell to her own father.

"Maarja!" I cry, but then quickly cover my mouth with my hand. Some of the men in my car wake up and stare at me as if I am crazy. The guard, who has probably also been dozing, stirs at his end of rail car.

But the little girl has disappeared once more.

I am sad that I was unable to catch a single one of those flowers. I would have preserved it even after everything else was stripped from me.

(Irkutsk, August 7, 1948.)

BAIKAL

It seems that they want our train to pass by Lake Baikal at night. However, it does not happen that way. An hour or two after leaving Irkutsk, we stop somewhere in the dark of night. There is no station, not a single light to pierce the darkness. On the right, I can sense a high black cliff, and on the left, an open space. A river roars in the distance.

August nights are not very dark or very long. We continue our journey at daybreak. It is then that we learn the reason for our stop. Part of the massive cliff had collapsed onto the tracks. The train crept slowly through this dangerous zone, where railway workmen cleared rocks and boulders from the roadbed with pickaxes.

Soon we arrive at the station building, where a sign reading "Baikal" hangs from the rafters. Behind the station is the harbor, and a lake as big as the sea.

Even if I knew the words to the song "In Siberia Beyond the Baikal," I could not sing it anyway. The pieces of coal, tossed in warning, would start clunking against the window.

And still, Baikal is an experience, even through the barred windows of our prisoner transport. We ride along the banks of the Baikal for almost the entire day. It is Sunday, August eighth. I read the Gospel from my New Testament to the men gathered around me, and we unite in silent prayer. The day shimmers with brilliant sunshine, and the Baikal is so blue that it seems as if the heavens have spilled all their azure into the lake. But there is not a single fisherman's hut standing on its banks, nor a single boat in its waters.

Barbed wire fences and red-epauletted guards with an automatic rifles stand by each bridge. Even the stations and the dwellings surrounding them have no other occupants other than security personnel.

It is as if we are riding along the banks of the Dead Sea. We see not a single sail, not a single boat, and not even the wind bothers to whip up waves on the water's surface.

On our right, the secrets of Siberia lie hidden behind a mountain. The hillside is dotted with oak trees. Frothy mountain streams cascade down its slopes. At times, steep cliffs loom directly in front of us. The engine chugs directly into the red granite. At the mouth of the tunnel, a gunman stands guard. We do not wave to him.

There are so many of these tunnels! The train slips through some of them in a few seconds, but in others, it is dark for so long that the ride becomes sinister.

The sun is already sinking as green meadows appear on the shores of Lake Baikal. Here we see our first fishermen, drawing fishing lines and nets into their boats. A fishing village stands not far from shore.

But then, the tracks turn away from the lake.

That night, we are welcomed by the lights of the Ulan-Ude Station. We park by a platform that is crowded with people despite the lateness of the hour. Most of the men have broad faces with high cheekbones. Under the light of an electric bulb, two who look like brothers stare at our transport for a long time.

"Mongols!" mutters the journalist, straining to look out the window.

"Our forefathers," I reply.

"So they say," admits the journalist. "But that was so long ago that even Adam and Eve can't remember it anymore."

We speak no more about our forefathers.

Apparently, we will be taken no farther tonight. The men fall into peaceful sleep.

(August 8-9, 1948.)

I BECOME MASTER OF THE BARREL

The enormous barrack by the Tartar Straits at the Vanino Transit Camp are called the "Station." Every transport train carrying a fresh load of deportees must pass through it.

I am certain that the barn-like building, a structure filled with three levels of bunks, has been a place of fear and terror for all newcomers.

One hot August morning, we reach the shores of the Pacific Ocean. I see potatoes being grown in the gardens surrounding the station, and I am gladdened by the hope of getting some fried potatoes here. I have saved a bit of lard at the bottom of a small box for this purpose. But soon, I will see this daydream collapse into ashes and dust. My box with its lard is stolen during our first bath, and I am not to enjoy the flavor of potatoes for nearly eight years.

The men exit the rail cars. Some are wearing short pants, as if visiting a vacation spot. They are immediately ordered to pull on long pants. I perspire heavily as I haul my clothing-stuffed backpack, because I am also wearing my winter coat in this hot weather. I had been arrested on the street, in cold weather.

By the time we arrive at the barracks, the men are tormented by a terrible thirst. And what do you know, a large barrel of water stands by the door. But a young man holding a stick has been stationed beside it. Anyone approaching the barrel to get a drink is whacked with the stick.

The men curse their circumstances and begin competing for the best bunks. I place my bag on the floor and boldly approach the barrel.

“Stand back, or I’ll whack you!” threatens the young galoot, raising his stick.

“Are you a free man giving orders here?” I ask him calmly.

“Idiot! I’m a prisoner, just like you are,” he replies.

“But then why are you striking your brothers? Let them have a drink.” Having said that, I pick up my bag once again.

However, there is so much shoving going on that I cannot move from my spot. I am terribly thirsty. I look back at the barrel. The guard has gone, leaving only his stick.

Now I am master of the barrel. I put my bag down again. Taking out a cup, I quench my thirst undisturbed. Then I call out to the men: “If you’re thirsty, come and get a drink!”

Immediately, the shoving subsides. The men form a line and every one of them can drink his fill.

(Vanino, Aug. 20, 1948.)

THE RUSSIAN GOD

I will never forget that first night at the "Station."

After getting our slop at the mess tent, we scramble back to our lodgings. All kinds of functionaries keep going in and out, some wielding sticks, some not. They rarely have any problems with our group of convicts, because we were a relatively calm lot. Here, we finally realize how many Estonian men have been ripped from the womb of their country and thrust to the mercies of the unfamiliar winds that blow here on the Pacific coast.

Upon hearing that a fresh prisoner transport of Estonians has arrived, the Latvians already at the camp come forward to greet us.

To my great surprise, I meet Evald Turgan at the "Station." The *sukas*[21] treat him with great respect, calling him "The Professor."

As conductor of the local transit camp orchestra and a violin player, he can move about the prison zone freely. He introduces us to another Estonian musician, Tormis, who is said to be an excellent accordion player. He is no less respected that Professor Turgan.

I had officiated at Evald Turgan's wedding and christened his daughters. Now, their domestic happiness has been shattered to bits. His wife is being held at a camp on the shores of the Arctic Ocean.

To celebrate the great joy of our meeting again, I give my old friend some warm underwear and a pair of wool socks. If I had known what was to come, I would have gotten rid of even more items from my bag.

21 *suka* – Criminal prisoners who collaborate with the Communists

Evald Turgan had been brought here from Kolyma because of his poor health. The few months he spent at Vanino had helped him regain his strength so well that he was afraid of being sent back to Kolyma. He told us of his life at the camp, which had been relatively tolerable because he had managed to spend all those terrible days working as a musician.

Before we are ordered to sleep, our guests must return to their barracks. Then comes the order that we always eagerly await, even in the cellar of Pagari Street, because it means that we can forget everything for eight hours; forget that we no longer have any freedoms, any rights. For eight hours, we can return home, embrace our loved ones, and be happy once more.

"Down for the night!" shouts one of the stick-wielding men. And all the prisoners must quickly scramble to their places. My bunk is right up under the ceiling. The air is thick up there, but I will never have to worry about feeling chilly.

That enormous shed soon resonates with the snoring of men exhausted by their strange experiences and strong emotions.

Suddenly, a shout from outside: "Help, help!"

I had just dozed off when the cry for help woke me. But not just me. All the men are up. Some are already climbing down from their bunks. The room buzzes with questions: "What's going on? Who's being hurt?" Before we can shake off the fog of sleep, several dozen boys storm into the barracks, knives and clubs in hand. Quickly, they disperse all through the room, bellowing at the top of their lungs in Russian: "Lie down!"

Our Estonian-speaking men have no idea what they are saying, and keep trying to get up, or just to see what is going on. The beating begins. A young Russian boy, eyes bulging and a knife in his teeth, climbs up to the third bunk where we are. "Lie down!" he screams, waving his knife as he nears us.

We follow his orders and lie there, holding our breath, waiting to see what will happen.

As the *sukas* realize that our flock of sheep is all too easy to subdue, they leave the barrack, one after the other. As he reaches the door, one of them sticks an axe in his bootleg.

I am bold enough to peer over the edge of the bunk once more. An older man, a member of our prisoner transport, is brought in, along with his suitcase. He is accompanied by two *sukas*. One of them has the top buttons of his shirt unbuttoned, and I see a cross necklace on his hairy chest and a knife handle sticking out of his bootleg. He must be one of the "peacemakers." Once they have escorted the old man to his place, the *suka* with the cross gives a speech. He says they have rescued one of our "compatriots" from robbers, and warns us not to plan any resistance. He promises to beat the would-be robber without mercy. He promises to bring the rogue to our barracks the following morning and beat him up in front of us.

He is a terrific speaker. When he has finished, he asks "Where is your interpreter?"

I call out: "Right here!"

"Well, go ahead, interpret what I said."

I interpret his lecture into Estonian. Since I have consented to be his mouthpiece, I dare to ask him a question: "Tell me, please, what is that cross around your neck?"

"This is the cross of the Russian God. I am a Russian man and I believe in the Russian God. Understand?"

"I also believe in God and in the crucified Jesus, our Savior. But if I dare to wear His cross around my neck, I would not dare to carry a knife in my bootleg."

The fine gentleman is not upset by my statement. He looks at me inquisitively, smiles slyly and says: "Well, go to sleep now, all of you. Good night!"

The next morning, the old man – Känd – tells us about last night's escapade. A half-breed from his rail car had betrayed him to the thieves, because he had refused to share any of his plentiful supplies with the boy. And the thieves had tried to steal all the poor man's belongings. They ordered him to step outside, and then tried to rip the suitcase with all its contents from his hands. Thanks to the commotion that arose in the barracks, they did not succeed. The one who had ordered him to step outside was that man with the cross.

Soon, our new "bosses" show up to resolve last night's incident.

Three *sukas* enter the barracks, this time without knives and clubs. Only God knows which one is the highest-ranking man. They ask Känd, as if in front of the judge's bench: "Can you identify the man who tried to take your suitcase?"

As a former teacher, Känd most certainly understands Russian and does not need an interpreter. But those functionaries cannot understand what he stutters in response. I must intervene once more.

Känd tells me plaintively: "The man who is now demanding my testimony is the one who tried to take my suitcase. How can I tell him that? He'll stab me to death."

"What's he saying? I want to know all of it!" the worshipper of the Russian God demands, sensing that something is amiss.

I say: "He says he was so confused with fear that he cannot remember the face of the thief."

"Well, well!" says the "judge" with relief. "But we caught the guy anyway." So saying, he punches one of the three boys in their gang. To our surprise, we recognize him as one of those who came to "calm us down" last night, knife in teeth.

And then, with a pious mug, the "judge" solemnly declares that the boy will receive his punishment here and now.

At that, the other two characters, who seem to be higher-ranking, grab the third *suka* by the scruff of the neck and drag him off into the attendant's room, which soon echoes with dark thuds and horrible screaming.

But when they have finished putting on this show behind closed doors, even the most slow-witted man among us realizes that this has been nothing more than a farce.

(Vanino Transit Camp, August 21, 1948.)

THIS ISN'T A FASCIST BATHHOUSE

During our time at the "Station," the men of our rail car are kept together.

They send us to the baths three carloads at a time, meaning a total of about 100 men.

Each time a new group of men is delivered to the bathhouse, the chief *suka* gives us a lecture that always begins: "You bums had better behave. I don't want any noise when you hand over your rag-bags for the roaster. Nobody's gonna steal anything from you. Nobody's gonna offend you. This isn't a fascist bathhouse. It's a Soviet bathhouse, which means it's completely different. You understand?"

At that, we are to answer in unison: "We understand."

But since we do this rather poorly, the chief *suka* makes us repeat it several times, to the great delight of the grinning hooligans around him. After were have listened to his admonitions and reassurances, we have to wait for the preceding group to leave the bathhouse.

As the day darkens, the air gets rather cool, despite the oppressive heat of the day.

Some of us crouch, some stand by our bags in the bathhouse yard. Suddenly, loud shrieks emanate from the bathing room. Half-naked and totally naked men stream from the room, followed by club-wielding men, who are beating them viciously. Suddenly, the entire yard is filled with *sukas*. It seems that each one is carrying a club as they surround the men from our train. The men are ordered to kneel right there in the muddy yard, where they are beaten mercilessly. The club-wielding guards are swearing and screaming as they thrash those poor naked men, none of whom offer up any resistance.

We keep a respectful distance, not having any idea of what happened in the bathhouse to bring this about.

Standing beside me, a Russian boy from our rail car declares: "So this is a Soviet bathhouse. It looks like you get some great steam from the rocks!" Later we learned that one of our men had shoved a barber after he had cut the prisoner while shaving his groin. All the barbers were *sukas*, men and women both. They shaved any and all hair they could find on the men's bodies.

This is a brutal lesson for us. At least we now know how we must behave in a Soviet bathhouse.

When the beating is over, they order the muddy and badly beaten men to get dressed. A few minutes later, they are brought outside again. Surrounded by a gauntlet of club-wielding guards, they are lined up, and even before they are taken away, an official shouts orders at us.

With heavy heart, I enter this glorious Soviet bathhouse, the one that offers pleasures like those I had just observed out in the yard.

In the foyer of the bathhouse barrack, we are met by a gang of red-faced punks who are all too eagerly reaching for our bags. The bathhouse overseer enters and orders us to tie our clothing to our bags. This means that those punks have to wait a while before they can ransack the contents of our pitiful bundles of belongings.

I have an awful lot of stuff, and no idea how to tie it into a proper bundle, especially since there is nothing to tie with. I use my underpants and shirt to tie my coat, blanket and jacket to the bag strap. All my belongings are tied together in this double bundle.

The men cast a suspicious eye at the punks who are so ready to pounce on our meager belongings. The bathhouse overseer notices this and offers some reassurance: "You don't need to be afraid. All your bundles will be sent through heat sterilization. Nothing will be lost. You'll get it all back right here, in good condition."

The men calm down. Leaving our belongings to the mercy of the thieving hooligans, we enter the baths. It is a large twilit room with a couple dozen showerheads. Each man is given a sliver of soap at the door. I do not take it, because I still have an untouched piece of soap that my wife had packed in one of the packages she had brought me in jail.

Before we can lather up, the men must take turns standing up on a stool. A full-lipped woman in a white coat, about 30-35 years old, grabs each man's penis, twisting it to the right and left, asking each one the same question: "Do you have crotch lice?"

Most of the Estonian men speak very little Russian, and cannot answer the woman's question. This makes her angry. She summons the bathhouse overseer, who once again calls us fascists. He finally adopts a reasonable tone and asks whether we have an interpreter. I step up to the woman and set about my familiar task. In addition to the simple questions about lice, the woman has other questions about ulcers and scars that she finds on the men's bodies. This female is evidently either a doctor or a surgeon's assistant.

After she has finished the checkups, the men must submit to the barber's knife. Those barbers demonstrate some fine professional skills indeed. In barely a minute, all the hair that has grown anywhere on our bodies over the course of thirty one days is scraped off. One barber specializes in shaving heads and chins, another fells the forests under our arms and around the crotch.

Only then may we wash ourselves. We must wash quickly, without lingering, because there are not enough showerheads for all of us. We manage to stand two or three at a time under the warm cascade pouring from the ceiling. It might have been a pleasant shower, if only there were not so much misery and wretchedness involved with it.

We are not allowed this pleasure for very long. The next shift is certainly waiting outside already.

The command comes soon enough: "Finish up!"

Anyone who fails to hear this command is destined to leave the bath with soap on his face or body, because shortly after the command is given, not another drop of water pours from the ceiling.

We are herded out of the bathhouse through a different door. Naturally, we are not allowed back into the room where we left our belongings, but must stand stark naked in the dark yard. The last of the new shift is already shoving its way into the bathhouse.

And now all hell breaks loose.

Our bags are scattered all across the yard. We pick them up, one by one, not finding the one that belongs to us. The men dart desperately from bag to bag, swearing and cursing, grumbling and wailing.

I stand there stark naked, feeling completely helpless amid the terrible commotion, not knowing what to do. The ground is beginning to freeze; I feel myself starting to shiver. Suddenly, in my helplessness, I recall an image from home: whenever my wife misplaced something; I tried to help her look for it, impatiently tearing the room apart. But she would simply stand there and pray. She would ask the Savior's guidance to show her where the lost object is. I always found it ludicrous that she would turn to God for such trivial affairs. But now, there is nobody else who can help me. And I do the same: I fold my hands in the direction of the swearing and cursing gaggle of men and pray: "Jesus, help me find my clothes."

Having said that, I walk calmly away from this pushing and shoving swarm of men, some of whom are already getting dressed. I am planning to lean against a trestle that is standing there. And I lean right onto my bag, which has been placed atop the trestle. All my clothes are there. I am missing only a few empty boxes. One had a little bit of lard left in it.

All right, let those fellows eat my Estonian pork fat. They deserve it for teaching us more in one evening than we could have learned over many years of just reading books about the realities of Soviet life.

(At the Vanino Transit Camp, August 21, 1948.)

YOU WILL GET YOUR THINGS BACK

After the baths, we are taken to an area where we are relatively free to move about from barrack to barrack. However, we may go outside the barbed-wire fence only to visit the outhouse.

The morning after the brawl at the bathhouse dawns sunny. This day promises to be nothing special. As far as the eye can see, there are nothing but barbed wire fences and barracks. Even so, as more and more prisoners are brought into the transfer camp, it is soon evident that the number of barracks is inadequate. Here and there, I see them housed in large Army tents. According to Evald Turgan, the Vanino Transit Camp has held more than 60,000 prisoners awaiting transfer to their final destination. Here, by the Tatar Strait, lies a huge warehouse of living goods, human equipment for the mines of Kolyma.

Because we were newcomers, the *sukas* focused most of their attention on us. They ran from barrack to barrack, looking for any kind of booty. They struck up conversations by asking us how we are feeling. They were interested in finding musicians and artists, as if we had all been brought here for a huge arts festival.

In our barrack, a singer, the diminutive Ants Känd, organized a men's choir, and even the *sukas* would attend the performances and praise the singing.

But now, in the morning after the bathhouse incident, an unfamiliar official, accompanied by two boys, enters our barrack and addresses us: "We have been hearing complaints about men losing some items in the baths. If anyone wishes to submit a claim for lost items, please come forward. Your items will be returned without fail."

"What's he saying?" the men shout. This announcement was made in such erudite terms that I had to rack my brain in order to translate it.

Many of the men had discovered a large number of items missing from their bags, but none dared to step forward. One peasant mumbled: "Once the bear gets something into his mouth, it's already up his ass. You won't be getting anything back." Another says: "Yeah, go ahead a make a claim. They'll just stab you to death."

Nobody dares to come forward.

I had given my bag a perfunctory inspection. I realized that my leather gloves were missing as well as my bakelite boxes. I am the first to step forward in hopes of retrieving my belongings. Emboldened by my courage, some other men also demand the return of their stolen property. There are eleven of us who follow that official to a barrack with tables, stools and long shelves stacked with books and files. Apparently, it is some kind of office. It also contains *sukas* of every caliber: large and small, some mere boys, some middle-aged men. They look at us without hostility. The official who escorted us sits down at the table and writes down our names. As he does so, one of our group sneaks out the door. The official makes a list of the items we claim to have lost in the "Soviet bathhouse."

After our complaints have been recorded, he calls some fellows, presumably bath attendants, over to the table, gives them the sheet and sends them to look for our things. They soon return with two bakelite boxes and a man's hat.

I claim the two boxes, and Mr. Loone, the schoolteacher from Tartu, takes his hat.

"And you found nothing else?" the official asks with feigned sternness.

"Nothing," the petty thieves affirm with a shrug.

"Well, as you can see, this is all we could find. Too bad. But we'll keep looking," assures this lovable *suka*.

As I start to collect my boxes from the table, a small boy from the band of *sukas* approaches me and says: "Mister, let me have that red box."

"Do you like it?"

"Yes, very much!"

"All right, you may have it."

And so, our attempts to retrieve our stolen property were rewarded with a hat and one bakelite box.

When I started stuffing my box into my bag, I was stunned to find my leather gloves. They had not been stolen after all. I had inconvenienced those thieves unnecessarily. But I was glad to get my box back, at least. It served me well as a cup during my time at Magadan.

(Vanino Transit Camp, Aug. 21, 1948)

WE STRIKE A BLOW WITH OUR BUNK BOARDS

At Vanino, we were never allowed to live in one barrack for more than two days in a row. Time and again, some *suka* would come by and order us to follow him to a different place.

One morning, we are taken to an area where the barracks are intermingled with tents. They open the door to an empty barrack for one hundred fifty men. Thanks to all this mixing, our group has become rather diverse. It is now a mixture of men transported from several places: Lithuanians and Latvians, Estonians and Ukrainians. Nearly all of them still have their own clothing and bags containing reserve supplies.

We have just managed to get settled on our bunks when the barrack door opens and seven men jump in. Without even the courtesy of a pleasant "Good morning," they get right down to business.

"All right, little men, pile up all your things right here," orders one of them in Russian, stroking the knife stuck into his bootleg.

"What do they want?" the Estonians ask.

"Our bags!" I explain.

Since we do not respond immediately to the orders given by the chief of the thieves, his lackeys jump into action. They pull out their knives and take a step toward us.

Some of the men closest to them lose their nerve and relinquish their bags. Having deposited their belongings, they are ordered to stand aside and let the rest of us do the same.

These knife-wielding thugs seem to be taking their job rather seriously. And yet, there are 150 of us to seven of them.

"Men, let's resist!" I whisper to my nearest compatriot.

"Quiet!" he says agitatedly. "Can't you see what they have in their hands? One of them also has an ax in his boot."

I leave my group and retreat to a far corner of the barrack. I try my luck with some other Estonians, encouraging them to resist. Since these men are not from my rail car, they did not witness how I already brought one stick-wielding thug to his knees. They do not trust me to lead any resistance. One of them reassures me: "Don't worry, they won't take everything. They'll take the stuff from the first bags they get and then they'll just go away." However, the prisoners continue to relinquish their belongings, without uttering a wingle word in protest.

A heavy-set Lithuanian whom I had spoken with the day before, and who had introduced himself as a boxer, glares darkly from his bunk behind the group at the events unfolding on the floor. I nudge him. With gestures rather than words, I indicate that it is a travesty to let these seven hooligans steal the last of our belongings.

"But how can we pull it off?" asks the Lithuanian.

Several loose planks on the bunks have already caught my eye. I point to them silently. The Lithuanian yanks at one and discovers it is not fastened at all. Without further ado, he grabs it and presses forward to the front of the crowd. I follow him with another plank.

The thieves are so engrossed in examining their booty that they are unaware of our plan to attack. They assume that someone is making his way up front to give up his bag.

As soon as the Lithuanian reaches the pile of relinquished bags, he swings his plank, quick as lightning, whacking the closest thug so hard on his head that he collapses onto his face and lies still.

Another thief springs forward, only to meet with a blow from my plank, but the force of my swing sends me flying onto my own back. As I get to my feet, I see the Lithuanian take a final swing at the last thief as he scrambles out the door after the others.

Our booty consists of a knife left behind by one of our guests.

We close the door and wait to see what will happen next. The barrack is deathly silent for some time, except for an occasional gurgle from the unconscious thief.

We wait, but nobody returns. My compatriots suddenly find their courage after the fact. Boastful talk and curses fill the barrack. Apparently, their spirits are slow to ignite, and only when the danger is long gone does their courage rise to the surface. I start to feel ever more reassured that many more of them will reach for loose planks if the thieves should ever invade again.

As they walk over to retrieve their bags, I instruct them: "These bags are now ours. Those who have not added their bags to this pile, please do so now." The men wonder whether to laugh at me or take me seriously.

The Lithuanian asks me what I am saying. After I translate for him, he waves me off and lies down on his bunk. He does not even have a bag.

When the prison camp guard comes to line us up for our meal, we report the incident to him. He seems to know about it already. He says: "No problem, we'll get rid of that snake soon."

By "snake," he means the thief we have killed.

When we returned to the barracks, he had been cleared away. We expected an investigation into the affair, but apparently this was such a common occurrence that nobody even cared. However, those thieves kept a respectful distance, even though we encountered them at close quarters many times.

(Vanino Transfer Camp, August 12, 1948)

MY MEETING WITH THE TUXEDOED MAN

The man who joined the chow line dressed in a soiled tuxedo had an expressive, highly intelligent face. Right after gulping down my food, I went over to him. The tuxedoed man was sitting on the edge of his bunk and breaking chunks of bread off a loaf, eating them with gusto. I sat next to the man to speak to him.

In a prisoners' barrack, people get to know each other and become fast friends rather quickly.

The stranger apologized for discarding his starched collar soon after his arrest, and for not having his vest dry cleaned for far too long. I realized that he had retained his sense of humor in spite of the circumstances. A very promising character, indeed.

I soon learned that he was a West German journalist who had been assigned to cover the opening night performance at the renovated opera house in East Berlin.

The State Security men had at least been courteous enough to let him watch the premier performance all the way to the end. But before he could applaud, they moved into the box to arrest him. Evidently, they had decided that his applause would be unnecessary. And now he found himself by the Tartar Sound.

"Fascinating, isn't it?" asked von Rosenberg with a smile, offering me a chunk of bread from his loaf. Not wanting him to be embarrassed about eating in my presence, I took my own loaf from my bag and broke off a few crumbs, occasionally popping one into my mouth.

And so we sat together on the edge of the bunk and chatted. We had lots to talk about. My German friend did not want to say much about his trip through Russia. It differed little from ours, but he had clattered along in the barred rail car for two days more than we had. He told me about Germany: how they are healing the wounds of war, how the economy is already in an upswing, and how their hopes for the future are high.

"But what's the use of all that, if you can't even be there?" I teased my enthusiastic interlocutor.

"Well, I am a journalist. Here, I plan to gather subject matter for some additional chapters to those communist-authored books describing the situation in this great Soviet land," he explained.

"What books do you mean? I don't know of any," I apologized naively.

"The first one I read was *'In der roten Hölle'* ('In the Red Hell'), written by some former Dutch communist," explained the tuxedoed man. He also mentioned the book by former Austrian communist, Captain Klug, entitled *"Das Verraten Sozialismus"* ("The Betrayal of Socialism"). I had seen that one during the German occupation, but unfortunately, had not read it.

He spoke most excitedly about a book by a German communist who had enthusiastically emigrated to the Soviet Union, where he spent a good deal of time slandering his homeland. Then, the communist found himself behind bars in this paradise of his dreams. Hitler secured his release, but then exiled him from his real homeland as well. This prompted the badly tormented, disappointed communist to write a book about his experiences in the Soviet Union, entitled *"Das Land der Grossen Lüge"* ("The Land of the Great Lie").

The tuxedoed man explained: "When I first read these books, I thought the authors were being arrogant and slanderous. But now, I myself have seen everything I once read about in those books. In my opinion, the authors were altogether too soft. Each of these books needs one more chapter, and I feel it is my duty to write that chapter. At any rate, the words I will use to describe this country will not be nearly as kind."

I have no idea what happened to the tuxedoed man. I do know what happened to his tuxedo. It is in a place where all of us were forced to leave behind our clothing, a tenuous memory of the life we lived in freedom so long ago. The bathhouse attendants at the Magadan Transit Camp were experts in robbing us blind. The *konvoi* took anything that was still wearable to the market in town and bartered it off.

I doubt that they got so much as a pack of cheap tobacco in exchange for the tuxedo. It still does not measure up to a warm quilted jacket.

I will never know if his valor was trampled into the muddy floor of the Magadan sanitation-check transit camp along with his tuxedo. At any rate, I have heard nothing about any additional chapters having been written for the books that were once penned in anger against this country, a country that has shattered the fantasies of the dreamers that once wrote about it with admiration.

(Vanino Transit Camp, August 1948)

NOGIN NUMBER THREE

Long tables, reminiscent of a marketplace, stand by the prison camp's barbed wire fence. That is where they search the prisoners designated for Kolyma. Nobody has ever said we would be sent to Kolyma. Two days ago, a prisoner transport filled with cripples arrived at our gate. The men from my barracks were sent to meet and assist them.

Three thousand men enter the camp gates. That is actually the wrong way to put it. They are actually the remnants of three thousand men: crippled, blind, dystrophic, tuberculous and ravaged by God-knows-what other diseases. Deemed unsuitable, they have been removed from Kolyma.

I help a young blind man through the camp gates. I can no longer contain my curiosity and ask him: "Please tell me how you became blind."

"When you get to Kolyma, you'll know," he says secretively.

"He rubbed his eyes blind himself," grunts a one-armed man, a drop dangling on the tip of his nose. He does not use his good hand to wipe it off.

"Is that true?" I ask dully.

"True or not, but if you ever need to blind yourself, use lots of powder from an indelible pencil," instructs the blind man.

"Would I have to swallow it?" I ask naively.

"Idiot! I can tell you're inexperienced. Once you get to Kolyma, you'll figure it out soon enough. You rub it into your eyes to escape from hell, even though it means you'll be blind," explains the man.

I am horrified by the thought.

"And how did you lose your hand?" I turn to the other man, who seems more eager to talk.

"I lopped it off myself," is the gruesome reply.

"But why?" I inquire.

"Once you get there, you'll understand why," answers the one-armed man.

There it is again: "Once you get there." Why would I ever be taken out there?

"There are so many cripples. Have they all escaped Kolyma in this manner?" I ask uneasily.

"Nearly all of them," both men assure me in unison.

I see a stump of a man rolling himself along on wheels. I wonder if he too is happy to have escaped from Kolyma with what is left of his life?

Kolyma, Kolyma, that name takes on a sinister ring.

I finally realize that the men who have been convicted under Section 10[22] of Article 58 and taken from the cells two days before the transport departed were actually the fortunate ones.

The tall teacher from Saaremaa, Konrad Raun, had cheerfully informed me that he would be serving the rest of his Section 10, Article 58 sentence at Karaganda.

But I had not been taken from that cell. Later, I learned that not one man of the cloth had been summoned. My journey and that of my colleagues was to end in Kolyma.

Immediately after the arrival of the cripples' transport train, the *sukas* became ever more diligent in our barracks. They tried to convince us to sell our belongings. They showed us rags that they would gladly give us in exchange. Apparently, our pending departure had come as a surprise even to them. It would disrupt their ability to steal the last of our belongings. But we refused all transactions. Until the last, the men were confident that they might be able to keep at least some of their possessions.

And now we stand before those long tables, where we are again forced to disrobe at the orders of red-epauletted members of the Communist Youth.

They find only one "suspicious" item on me – my New Testament. A soldier tosses it onto the table. But I muster an authoritative demeanor and tell him: "You may not take this away from me."

---

22 *Section 10* – "Law" forbidding "propaganda and agitation Article 28 against the USSR" under which Stalin imprisoned Christians and others who did not follow his beliefs

"How's that?" the soldier asks, surprised.

"That is a Bible, and I have permission to carry it with me," I explain.

"We'll see about that!" is the *Komsomol* member's somber reply. He takes my property over to an officer and explains the nature of the book to him. I stumble along behind, pulling up my pants.

"Are you a cleric?" asks the officer.

"Yes, I am," I reply without hesitation.

The soldier is told: "He is permitted to take the book along."

So I am right after all, at least in the Vanino Transit Camp. Because of that, I remember the gang that sent us off with some fondness. However, we had experienced the other side of life at Vanino as well.

After four thousand men are methodically stripped of their belongings, we are taken outside the gates. We sit on a hillside above the Tartar Strait, with the Sakhalin Mountains rising in the background. They seem so much closer than the 80 kilometers I had measured on the map.

We are surrounded by a large group of gunmen. Occasionally, an officer comes by to look us over. We are forbidden to speak, but we may enjoy the scenery all we want.

And so we wait. None of us have any idea what we are waiting for. Will a train take us to Sovgaran? Perhaps we are waiting for the train. Perhaps the next leg of our journey will take place on a ship. Our curious questions go unanswered. As darkness falls, a realization dawns. Apparently, the *chekists* are afraid of the people in the free workers' settlement. Somebody might count the number of prisoners and tell the Americans about it. Anything could happen. There could be spies anywhere.

Actions that fear the light of day must be carried out in darkness.

Apparently, the officers who searched us have fulfilled their plan ahead of schedule. And we must wait. Four thousand men sit around idly. I think – if we had spent this half a day working instead of sitting on the hillside, we might have accomplished more than just a little bit. However, in this glorious Soviet land, God gives plenty of time for accomplishing something, but the authorities are chronically short of bread.

And nobody tells the authorities to pay any of us a day's wages. They take whatever they can from us, giving us only meager rations of bread in exchange.

Finally, after the sun sets behind us and the evening chill makes us shiver, our work brigade is ordered to get up. Once again, they check to see if any men in the five-deep rows are missing. The command roars from several dozen throats: "Get a move on!"

Suddenly, we are surrounded by so many red-ribboned and gold-epauletted cowboys that we are gripped by fear.

The soldiers walk in silence, automatics at the ready. The officers shout and bark at our herd at the top of their lungs. Most of them carry truncheons, which they use rather generously.

The road is rugged, dotted with stumps and rocks. The men plod along in the dark, carrying their bags. Whole rows trip and fall. Those who obstruct the march in this way are beaten about the shoulders with the truncheons. The air is thick with curses of "You f---ing rats!" which darken the sky above our heads like a flock of crows. An officer of my own height walks alongside me for some distance, truncheon in hand. Unfortunately, I am on the outside of the column. My heavy bag is becoming a real nuisance. I curse myself for not having bartered it off to the *sukas*, or even given it away for free. Sticky sweat pours down my body. My feet are refusing to cooperate. I trip many times, but manage to stay on my feet. Suddenly, the man behind me trips and falls against me. I sprawl to the ground, followed by my bag. Horrible screams of "mother f...er" pierce my ears. As I struggle to rise, I see only the leather glove that has delivered a powerful blow to the nape of my neck. I am unable to get up very fast because of my disgusting bag, and I make contact with that leather glove once again. I have no time to suspect that the glove may be the one that was stolen from my bag, since I receive another, even more painful blow to the center of my back. Someone helps me up. I have to run to catch up to those in front of me.

"Close ranks," someone yells from somewhere. Again, the thud of beatings. This trek, punctuated by shrieked curses and blows from truncheons, is about two kilometers long. Out of breath, we reach the shores of the bay.

A large black ship lies at the dock.

We are herded down to the harbor without stopping.

We realize that our destination is indeed Kolyma. My second prophetic dream is coming true. It is the one I dreamed on the prisoner transport train:

A large group of men is gathered in a harbor somewhere. Before us rises the face of a cliff, behind us is the sea. An authority figure appears and begins handing out assignments. Each man, after receiving his assignment, leaves. I am left completely alone. Everyone else has vanished. In my dream, I do not know where I should go. Suddenly, Veskimäe, that "bandit" from Märjamaa whom I met in Cell 47 at Patarei Prison, walks up to me. He says: "Haamer, what are you waiting for?"

"Nobody needs me," I tell him sadly.

"You fool! Didn't they tell you that you're supposed to go and entertain children?" says Veskimäe.

"Entertain children?" I am so surprised by the job given to me in my dream that I wake up.

And now the expansive sea lies before us. But no cliff towers over the harbor. Soon I will reach my destination and take up my new job – entertaining children.

But our feet are still on the docks of Vanino on the mainland, from which the Pacific Ocean and the Sea of Okhota will separate me for nearly eight years.

Apparently, the loading of the ship is being delayed by some kind of confusion. Our column is not advancing.

We are ordered to sit. We are given a gruesome warning: anyone who stands up will be shot.

Silent as mice, 4,000 miserable men sit on the harbor dock and wait. Suddenly – movement. The *konvois* tighten their grip on their weapons. Something is going on up front. Many gold-epauletted figures dart forward past us. Someone shouts: "Don't stand up!" All the *konvois* repeat the order, their faces filled with rage. But we have no intention of standing up. Finally, the news about what has happened is passed along in whispers: "One of the Latvians jumped into the sea." Turning our heads ever so slightly, we pass the word all the way to the last rows.

We hear no more about the event. Only later do we learn that the Latvian was pulled out alive. Unfortunately, the man knew how to swim.

I sit right at the edge of the dock. Only one step more, and I can jump into the sea. I am so tempted by this opportunity that my soul is prepared to settle its accounts with my earthly life. I can not hold back this deluge of dark hopelessness. Kolyma is reputed to be hell. Only the horrible cripples, like the 3,000 men who had entered the gates of our camp day before yesterday, have any hope of escape. Could I chop off my own hand, or let frostbite take my fingers and toes, or would I have the fortitude to rub the sight out of my eyes with ink powder? Why suffer such torture, when freedom is right here for the taking?

I let my coat fall from my shoulders and stand up. Suddenly, a hand grabs my pants leg and pulls me back down.

"Are you crazy?" hisses the man next to me. "They'll shoot you!"

I sit back down. Apparently the *konvoi* did not see me. It is quite dark. Only dim twinkles of light emanate from the ship. I close my eyes. My soul protests against my return to life. I do not want to cry, but the tears force their way into my eyes. I have never been so totally miserable during all my time in prison.

I seek solace from the night. A part of me wants to pray, but I am unable to do so. I want to die, but someone's hand pulls me back. I feel the dread that accompanies arrival at the edge of despair.

And suddenly, a little boy's voice calls to me, as if in great distress: "Daddy, daddy!"

The voice is so clear that I look around. But all I see is a somber, shaggy mass of men hunched low to the ground.

I repeat the call: "Daddy, daddy!" And now I recognize it as the voice of my eldest son Eenok, who was ill when I left home.

"Eenok," I whisper. "You came to console your daddy. Your daddy must never again be so miserable. Never again, do you hear me!"

I make a promise to my son on that dock in Vanino. Suddenly, my heart is lighter. I am able to pray again.

Now I am prepared for anything, come what may.

Already they are ordering us to get up. We shuffle toward the ship's gangway. That large, somber cargo ship has the name *Nogin* written on its side. To this day, I have no idea who this Nogin is, nor have I cared whose name is borne by this slave ship. Perhaps he was a *chekist* like Felix Dzerzhinski, whose name graced another slave ship sailing the same route. I heard about that in Vanino. Our transport across the Okhota Sea went down into Soviet slave route history as "Nogin Number Three," since this was its third trip this year from Vanino to Kolyma.

When we reach the ship's gangway, we are drawn into an unexpected dance. For no apparent reason, young hoodlums wearing red epaulettes stand on either side of the gangway screaming a single command: "Hurry up!" Anyone who does not understand the meaning of the term is given a full translation with the help of a stick.

It is very hard for me to jog up the gangway with my heavy bundle. But I manage, because someone is walking beside me, encouraging me with his whisper: "Daddy, daddy, be brave." Breathless, we reach the deck. I follow in the tracks of men jogging ahead of me. We cannot deviate from our path, because our route takes us through a gauntlet of club-wielding thugs with red epaulettes. A heavy cable lies underfoot by the trapdoor leading to the ship's hold. The men who trip over it are encouraged to get up with several whacks of a stick. Two savages wearing *Komsomol* emblems stand there with clubs, shouting "Faster, you f---ing fascists!" My feet catch the cable. I fall into a sprawl, bundle and all. But I scramble to my feet again before they can beat me. In front of me, a man falls down the ladder into the hold. I have lost my bundle. It is being trampled underfoot. I am about to trip again. I cannot reach my bundle, because blows from a stick force me to jump down into the hold. I manage to grab onto the handrail as I am pushed downward by a man falling down the ladder toward me. Still, I wait by the ladder to see if someone will throw down my bundle. But the only things being thrown down are men. I try to help, try to keep them from falling onto the iron floor of the hold. Finally, my bag is tossed down as well.

An old cabin boy like me knows that the process by which they loaded this ship violates every single maritime law. Even animals are treated much more humanely. But here, we are not human. At least not in the opinion of those thugs with their red epaulettes.

They pulled the Latvian out of the water because every man has to be accounted for. Every slave represents an investment. However, these kids with their sticks have not the slightest regard for any type of investment. They treat us as if we were mere logs. When all has fallen silent up above, we start hearing the moans of men in the hold among us. One of our group is a Ukrainian surgeon who attends to each moaning man.

Two men have broken ribs, one has a broken collarbone, another has all his fingers twisted backwards. I can no longer remember how many others had sprained, twisted and bruised limbs.

But nobody punishes the *chekists* for their acts of sabotage.

And so, we set out on our long voyage across the sea, our prospects nothing but miserable.

But the ship was strong and sure. A brass plate fastened to the wall read: "Made in U.S.A. Illinois."

(Vanino, August 26, 1948)

THE TRANSIT

In that dreary ship's hold, a rumor was being passed from bunk to bunk: we are being taken to a Japanese island. Someone claimed to see a lighthouse beacon on the right.

We were forbidden to climb from the hold up to the deck at night. Some of the men did so anyway. Apparently, the guards on deck were asleep.

The Ukrainians huddled together, deep in discussion. Most of the hold slept.

On the first day, I had already met one Catholic and one Orthodox priest. I translated some parts of the New Testament for them. We chatted and prayed. The Orthodox priest was serving a ten-year sentence, the Catholic priest Dr. Ivanjuk was serving twenty five. Both had been sentenced under Section 10 of Article 58.

I had also approached a Jew from Ukraine who was holding a book of English grammar. He was happy to take advantage of my poor English vocabulary to enrich his even poorer English language skills.

I cannot say I was bored. Besides, I was trying to raise the spirits of my countrymen, since most of them were terribly dispirited.

On the bunk next to me lay an Estonian Army cavalry officer (I think his name was Jaan Sutt). He was being transported to Kolyma to serve the last two years of his five-year sentence. I started reading to him about the Acts of the Apostles, and my readings soon evolved into a Bible study for all my countrymen.

On the very first night of our voyage, he entrusted me with a secret. He had been approached by one of the Ukrainians who felt he would be the most suitable man to encourage the Estonians to take part in an uprising they were planning. A group of Ukrainian *Banderas*[23] had devised a peculiar scenario: the night we sailed closest to Japan, they would attack the guards and force the ship to change its course toward freedom.

When I heard about it, I was mad with excitement. But soon, I was overwhelmed with doubt. How could we resist automatic weapons bare-handed? We could see guards standing by machine guns each time we went topside to the latrine. I was sure those weapons might also be used against us.

Above all else, Sutt feared that this might be a provocation. He had already had some bad experiences with Ukrainians, and was hesitant to join their scheme. However, what he did after that was completely uncalled for. Shortly after our conversation, he climbed up on deck and betrayed the Ukrainians' conspiracy to the officers above. I did not find out until the next morning, when the coast of Japan was already far behind us.

As I awoke, I immediately noticed that the trapdoors to the hold stood open, with the barrel of a machine gun peering through each one. For the last seven days of our voyage, nobody was allowed on deck any more.

An enormous pot had been placed directly under one trapdoor. Climbing up there to relieve ourselves was rather tricky. This pot was used for seven days by 400 men. During that time, it was never emptied. Day by day, the air became heavier with the stench of urine and vomit. To add insult to injury, a storm rose on the Okhota Sea. That restless sea is hardly ever still at this time of year. And now, in that stuffy hold, nearly all the men became seasick.

As the ship pitched and rolled, the men tried to lie on their bunks, but they were immediately overcome by seasickness. The fortunate ones made it to the pot to vomit. The odor of ammonia emanating from that container made us even more nauseated.

The trapdoor to the deck was opened only at mealtimes, so that a kettle of fish soup could be passed through. However, none of the men had

23 *Banderas* – Nickname given to people from Western Ukraine

bowls. We shared the few cups that remained. The ship rolled so hard that the soup sloshed over the edge of the kettle onto the floor. Nobody bothered to clean it off the floor of the hold. The rotting soup just added to the horrible stench. Many men no longer had the energy to get up for meals. The younger, more robust men would wolf down several portions at once. However, it never stayed down for long. Usually, it would come right back up, undigested.

A rosy-cheeked Russian boy sat on the edge of his bunk, eating with gusto. He was delighted to receive any extra uneaten portions. He had probably never fared as well as he did now, in the stinking hold of the *Nogin*. Suddenly, he started to cry and his face paled. He got up, but before he could reach the latrine pot, he vomited his entire meal onto the iron floor of the hold. Someone near him cursed resignedly: "Hey, watch your f---ing mouth." In this ship's hold, this was the prayer of thanks for a hearty meal.

I have always loved the sea and sailed its waters, but any romantic nostalgia about a sailor's life died forever in that hold. And yet, I never succumbed to seasickness. I ate so little that there was nothing to bring back up. I took it upon myself to take water to those lying on their bunks. By keeping busy, I had no time to get sick, although I felt my strength waning day by day.

The end of our voyage was particularly horrible. The latrine pot started to overflow, and the stench in the hold became unbearable. Most of the men no longer rose from their bunks. The thieves among us got down to work, but many of the men had already become so apathetic that nobody resisted the robbery. Only when they tried to rip a weakened old man's gold teeth out of his mouth did a threatening rumble arise in the hold.

According to our estimations, it was early in the morning of September 3 when the *Nogin* bumped against a wharf. Soon after that, they began to unload us.

As we emerged from the hold into daylight, I was speechless with astonishment. We had arrived at the harbor I had seen in my dream. That massive cliff stood right here, almost within arm's reach.

It was about four kilometers from the harbor to Magadan. It was too hard for me to walk the distance. I needed the support of two men. And yet, I managed to carry my own heavy bag for one last time.

(On the trip to Magadan, Aug. 26 - Sept. 3, 1948)

I AM GIVEN MY FIRST FUFAIKA[24]

A bathhouse stands somewhere at the edge of the city of Magadan. Its courtyard is large enough to accommodate several thousand men. Its function is to provide the loads of transport prisoners a thorough scrubbing, as well as allow every last shred of their belongings to be stolen.

They make us sit and wait in that bathhouse courtyard, because not all the men can fit under the showers at once, nor can everyone's clothes could fit into the roaster, although not many members of that last prisoner transport have made it to the baths.

The gateway to the yard has a red cross painted on it, with the word *Sanpropusk*[25].

We soon realize that there is very little in this place that can dignify this symbol of mercy, the red cross.

As we wait our turn, various rumors percolate about what we can expect in the baths. Someone says that any new clothes will be stolen, and busies himself with sewing patches onto the knees of his pants. Another claims that clothes in good condition will be the ones we will manage to keep, and tears off the patches he sewed on at Vanino.

I have all kinds of clothes, and no idea what I should do with them. I look them over, feeling as if I am seeing them for the last time. I put on the sweater onto which I had woven "Maiki"[26]in gray letters while riding the train. Back in Vanino, they had thought I was a sailor, and that "Maiki" was

24 *fufaika* – Quilted jacket; a prisoner or ex-prisoner dressed in one

25 *Sanpropusk* – Sanitation entrance

26 *Maiki* – Pastor Haamer's nickname for his wife Maimu

the name of the last ship that I had sailed. I never want to take that sweater off again, not until it falls apart and crumbles off my back. We are ordered to take our bundles and go to the baths.

No sooner have we stepped in the door than the terrible shouting and name-calling begins. Flush-faced bath attendants shout "Get undressed! Hurry up!" punctuated by all the requisite obscenities. We must to relinquish everything that the bath attendants take a liking to. If you resist, they pick up their sticks. A red-epauletted man stands by, watching calmly. He does not care to get involved. Undoubtedly, the thieves give him his fair share. Without exception, the bath attendants are all "friends of the people" who have been thrown into prison.

Because they lack the language skills, the Estonian men are unable to say a single word in their own defense. A bath attendant tosses their good clothes to the floor with a single scornful word: "Junk!" If they try to protest in their own native language, the bath attendant shrieks with rage: "Shove it up your ass!" End of conversation.

They do not have such an easy time with me. I turn directly to the red-epauletted man and ask how he can watch this shameless pilfering with such calm. At my question, he scratches at his pants as if in pursuit of fleas, but does not say a word. At the same time, the bath attendant is pulling my shirt and pants out of my bag, throwing them onto the floor as "junk" and casting an appraising eye at my woolen blanket. Instead of tossing it on the floor, he puts it aside. I say to him: "That blanket should be enough for you. Please, at least leave me the coat. I am ill." At that, the thief looks up and throws the coat at me, along with a trolley hook that he has picked up off the floor, and says: "So take it and go!"

That is his way of saying I should not try to claim any other items.

And so I am forced to surrender all my belongings, even my "sailor's" sweater.

I recognize the trolley hook from my Patarei Prison days. I stuff my empty bag and my coat into it. All I have left of the clothing that I brought from home is my coat. I hand my hooked belongings over to another bath attendant, who carries them into the roaster.

I take another brief look around the room. Plunder and robbery is in high gear. Suddenly, I notice that my chrome-leather boots and felt boots have been set down next to each other. Without a word, I grab both pairs and scamper into the shower room.

Fortunately, I have enough presence of mind to also grab my New Testament, empty wallet, leather gloves and some handkerchiefs. Just in case.

I stuff them all into a chrome-leather boot and start washing myself with the sliver of soap that was shoved into my hand at the bath chamber door. But my eyes are glued to the felt and chrome-leather boots by the shower room wall. Suddenly, a naked man stops at that spot and makes a grab for my chrome-leather boots. But I am faster. I take a few running steps toward the thief, but he has already noticed me. Realizing that he is outnumbered by the Estonian-speaking men in steamy room, he flees without a word. After that, I hold the footwear in one hand as I lather and rinse with the other, just in case.

Now I must submit to the barber, and entrust my meager belongings to the care of one of my countrymen.

But the barber has a terrible time cutting my hair. He starts with one pair of clippers, which do nothing but tangle my thin hair. The enraged barber uses the clippers to yank out more hair than he cuts. Then he tries another pair of clippers. They are even worse. My hair is so fine that it refuses to submit to those clippers as well. Shouting obscenities, he yanks about half the hair out of my head, and sends me on my way with a punch to my scruff. I do not care. I have no hair on the top of my head anyway. And now the few wisps I have left might provide me with a little warmth.

After the barbers have finished their work, clothing is distributed. We are given underwear at one counter, pants, a long military field shirt and a *fufaika* (quilted jacket) at another, and cap and boots from a third.

Shorter men have it easy. They can take anything tossed to them and make it fit. For me, it is a different story. The old man handing out underwear calmly finds me the largest size of underwear they have. The field shirt fits me, but is too short to cover my abdomen. The quilted jacket is so short that it barely reaches my navel. The top part of my chrome-leather boots will cover my shins, which are left bare by the inadequate pants. Although the boots they heave at me are the largest size available, they would not fit on my feet even if I cut a piece off my big toe. And instead of my own good ski cap, I am given a Russian-style woolen cap with a narrow visor. To make it fit my head, I have to rip open the back seam and restitch it with bits of string.

Now I am dressed.

I do get my coat back from the roaster. It covers all the insufficient lengths of my prison uniform. I step into line with all the other *fufaikas*, like some kind of functionary. I lend my rescued felt boots to a tall man who is shifting from one bare foot to another. Then, they line us up between rows of guards holding automatic weapons, flashlights glowing at us like watchful eyes.

There are at least another three kilometers to go until we reach the actual prison camp.

The barefooted men feel the pain of this journey most acutely, because the night is already bringing freezing temperatures.

(September 4, 1948 in Magadan.)

IN THE "PULPIT" ONCE MORE

The entire population of our prison camp is taken to the bathhouse every ten days. Gunmen surround the nearly 1,000 men. One soldier, carrying a red flag, walks in the lead, and another brings up the end, to make sure that no vehicle convoys drive into us. For me, the procession is always a festive one, because I have never marched behind a red flag before. At least I have something to cover my shoulders with. I still have my felt boots, although my coat now adorns a Ukrainian doctor who prances around the prison showing it off. To keep myself warm, I wear the field shirt and pants he gave me to wear over my other clothing. A compatriot of mine who had been assigned to sort our stolen clothing found my ski cap and the briefs with my name sewn into them. He retrieved them and brought them to me. My bundle of possessions also includes the cap I altered by basting the back seam together with string. I must keep it in case I needed to exchange it. The same goes for my ski cap. Who knows what kind of headgear I might get in exchange for it? Winter is approaching. If I have to rip my winter hat apart at the back, I will be in a bad way.

My galoshes have not been stolen yet. They too are in my bag, waiting to be exchanged for winter footwear.

Each time, those three kilometers from the prison camp into town represent a journey of humiliation. The *chekists,* shouting a never-ending string of obscenities, manage to make the trip so vile that I would rather endure the lice than march from the prison camp to the bathhouse.

Silent, *fufaika*-clad people watch us by the roadside. They have all been prisoners like us. Every time they see men or women like us, surrounded by gunmen, they recall their own experience. Finally released from the camps, they have stayed in this land which they have made habitable with their own blood, sweat and toil. The towns of Kolyma have been built by prisoners. Magadan is also the product of prisoner labor: prisoners paved the roads, prisoners mined the metals from the depths of the earth, prisoners built the factories for the enrichment of ore, prisoners lay the foundation for free men and women to earn their rubles. In a word, the existence and fortunes of the Soviet system in Kolyma rely entirely on the slave labor done by prisoners. We have been brought here to take the place of those who have perished in this slavery. Great are the numbers of those who were forced to live and work in inhuman conditions until 1949, in many such places, until Stalin's death.

Kolyma is an terrible land, to put it simply. We heard many stories about the lawless camps with their arbitrary rules, where only the strongest and greediest survive. We heard stories about a commander in the Dalstroy Camp System who personified this arbitrariness. Once day, he had decided to conduct an inspection. At one camp, after getting the prisoners lined up, he ordered: "Anyone who has surpassed his production plan, step forward!" When those men who had been praised for surpassing their planned production quota stepped forward, the commander took them all behind the prison camp and had them shot.

Word traveled swiftly from camp to camp. This Dalstroy commander does not like it when people surpass their production quota!

He went to another camp. Again, the men were lined up for inspection. "Anyone who has surpassed his production plan, step forward!"

Nobody stepped forward. At that, the brute ordered every tenth man to step out of line. These men were taken out behind the prison camp and shot.

Now, all of Kolyma is terribly confused. Nobody can guess what this sadist really wants. Apparently, he wants nothing more than to satisfy his thirst for blood. The prisoners exist to satisfy his thirst.

One day, he was hanged for being an "American spy."

There is nowhere to escape from this land. We heard stories about a camp somewhere by the Indigirka River, in which the prisoners organized an uprising, butchered the guards, and started moving eastward. Most of them perished in the tundra. But about one hundred men reached the Bering Strait. They struck a deal with the Chukchis, who promised to take them across the Bering Strait to Alaska. However, not a single one of them made it. They had not believed that the Chukchis might betray them. As soon as they stepped onto the ice of the Bering Strait, they were surrounded by Soviet border guards. Not one man survived.

In our camp, a Latvian officer succeeded in hiding himself behind an uprooted stump while hauling fuel to the prison camp. His absence was not noticed for three days. He never returned. I truly doubt that he managed to evade the bloodhounds who sniffed excitedly at the stump-filled area by the mountain camp, and then, bellowing hideously, ran off to pursue the scent.

Our feet now tread this terrible land, where the bear acts as prosecutor and any hope of humane treatment must be forever forgotten.

And yet, they will not have us be infested with lice.

To that end, we march to the bathhouse every ten days. The convoy commander has lectured us about the necessity of walking with dignity, arms linked. without looking around or behind us. However, the thieves among us choose to ignore these admonitions. They run between us, across the lines, anywhere they want. The armed guards shout their entire vocabulary of curses and obscenities at them, rattling the automatic weapons hanging on their shoulders, but to no avail. Instead, they swear and curse at the people trying to give the prisoners bread and tobacco.

I too refuse to obey their orders. I look around as much as I want. I am most captivated by Magadan Bay, which lies at the foot of the mountain, its water gray, as if someone were constantly rinsing dirty laundry in it.

Not all of us fit into the bath chamber at once. However, by the time darkness falls, our whiskered faces are cleaner, our quilted jackets and field shirts have been put through the roaster, and we are wearing clean underwear. I feel like a different person.

But the trip to the bathhouse is not without problems. A prisoner fails to fetch his clothes, held in a bundle on the trolley hook as they emerge from the roaster, quickly enough. And his clothes are gone. The thieves are always keeping a watchful eye for any opportunity to steal something. Nobody gives you new clothes; you might as well march back to the camp naked. My countrymen become anxious when the attendants start calling out the numbers on the hooks. They know the number of the hook on which their quilted jacket was roasted, but they have to guess what

When the shutter is opened, I step onto the platform where the trolley hooks with the clothes are tossed. As soon as the bath attendant calls out the number in Russian, I repeat it in Estonian. Each man rushes up to get the bundle that belongs to him.

When they call my number, I place the bundle under my foot until the last number is called. Only then do I have time to dress myself.

"That was the best sermon I ever heard," an old forest warden says to me. "When you stood up there calling out the numbers, I felt as if you were standing in a pulpit."

"But I was wearing my birthday suit," I laugh.

"But it is not your robe that gives the sermon; it is your heart that does the talking."

As a reward for this "sermon of the heart," I am given a patched shirt. The better ones have all been taken.

(Magadan Transit Camp, September 1948.)

“I’M THE DOCTOR HERE!”

“Who needs to go to the outpatient clinic?” shouts the attending officer. A few men elbow their way toward the door.

Do I need to go too? Perhaps I should tell them about some of my problems. Most important of all, I will get to walk a little.

Although it is not particularly cold outside, I pull on the overcoat that I still have and join the line of men going to the clinic.

But my vanity costs me my overcoat.

The clinic is only a few dozen meters away, and I could have made the trek in my field shirt. I do not know why the spirit possessed me to leave my quilted jacket on a hook, guarded by one of my countrymen, and go out showing off my overcoat instead.

Gleb Nikolajevich, who had been a mere surgeon’s assistant on the ship, has suddenly become a doctor. He sits in the attending officer’s room of the inpatient hut and receives the sick. As they step over the threshold into his office, each man doubles over and starts to moan. Only those with serious ailments behave with dignity. But those men are few and far between.

“Doctor, help me!” and again – “Doctor, help me!” they howl, holding their stomach with both hands, hoping to be admitted to the inpatient section, hoping to win a little more idle time in the transit camp.

The “doctor” is pleasant. He listens patiently to each man’s complaints, dispenses his so-called medicines, and admits the most annoyingly persistent ones to the inpatient section.

I am one of the last to see the doctor.

Gleb Nikolajevich pays keen attention to me. He lets me recount all my problems and ailments in detail. But his eyes drift to the overcoat that I have laid on the bench. Before he gives me my medicine, he looks behind the door to see if any more patients are waiting to see him.

He asks the two men who are still waiting their turn to come in. Before either one can say a word, he gives each one a tablet. Without further ado, he sends them away and turns his attention to "treating" me.

"You have a nice overcoat. Let me have it!" the dear, pleasant doctor says abruptly.

"What do you mean? I am a sick man, with weak lungs. I will catch a chill without my overcoat," I complain.

"You probably don't go outdoors very often, so you really don't need this overcoat. Besides, I could admit you to the inpatient section."

"I am especially cold when I am sleeping. My blanket was stolen in the bathhouse. This overcoat is the only warm thing I have left to cover myself with."

"All right, if you give me the overcoat, I'll get you a blanket in its place."

"But my pants are shabby. They reach only halfway down my calf," I persist.

"I'll get you pants too, and a field shirt as well," offers Gleb Nikolajevich.

In exchange for all these promises, I relinquish my overcoat to the doctor. This coat has kept my body warm for ten years, and now I must part with it when I need it the most. I remove the photos of my wife and children that I have sewn into the collar. Gleb Nikolajevich stretches out his hand and says, moved: "I can see you are an educated and sensible person. You will not regret this." To convince me of his sincerity, he gives me a few drops of valerian, a treat saved for a select few. He saves the valerian for the camp's most ridiculous hypochondriacs, who will soon be coming by for their dosage.

I return to my barrack in shirtsleeves.

The following morning, I am transferred, along with the few meager belongings I have left, to the inpatient section. My illness is registered as a "heart ailment." I have officially become a cardiac patient. My place is on a high bunk next to a jaundiced Ukrainian. We share one bed in the truest sense of the word, because when we get cold, we huddle together. One quilted jacket covers our shoulders, the other, our legs.

On the third day, Gleb Nikolajevich brings me a field shirt and pants. He has probably snitched them from some warehouse, because he also serves as the labor camp's health inspector.

Not until a few months later does old Kovalenko, the man who slept next to me in the "underground" workshop, extract a blanket from him. How he did so will forever remain a mystery.

Our dear, white-coated doctor now makes his rounds from camp to camp with my overcoat across his shoulders. A true gentleman.

I am bored just lying around on the bunk. I look for something to occupy my time. Once again, it is Gleb Nikolajevich who gives me something to do. I am to become a surgeon's assistant.

A tall, young, very intelligent student from the Leningrad Technical School is already working as the surgeon's assistant. His job is very simple. When Gleb Nikolajevich finishes receiving his patients, Ivan Ivanovich brings out two thermometers. One is for those on the left-side bunks, the other for the inhabitants of the right-side bunks. After each man has held the thermometer under his armpit for the designated period, Ivan Ivanovich notes the temperature on a sheet of paper. Since there are only two thermometers, this process is relatively tedious, although the time allotted for each man is strictly limited. Once everyone's temperature has been taken, Ivan Ivanovich barks: "Diarrhea sufferers!" All those complaining of diarrhea line up. Each one is given one gulp of potassium permanganate solution from a small glass. Then he orders: "Angina sufferers!" From this same glass, the men with sore throats are to gargle with the potassium permanganate. Then comes: "Heart ailments!" These patients are usually given an aspirin tablet, because no other medications are available. Patients with open sores take turns going into the doctor's office to rinse their wounds with the potassium permanganate.

Only those with erysipelas and jaundice are left alone.

One day they discovered that both these diseases are contagious, and they transferred the contagious patients to the bunks on the left wall of the barracks, leaving everyone else on the right.

I paid close attention to the procedures for processing and treating the sick, and was confident that I would prove to be a capable medical worker. Humbly, I took on the lesser title of "orderly," although the barracks were kept in order by the duty officer whose pay consisted of an additional bowl of soup.

When Ivan Ivanovich failed to show up at all one day, it looked like I would indeed become the doctor's actual assistant. My countryman Teras was lying in the "contagious diseases ward." The terrible hardships that he had suffered had left his whole body and soul completely drained. His breathing rattled terribly, and I feared he might have pneumonia. But Teras did not complain of pain, and his temperature was not especially high, leading Gleb Nikolajevich to diagnose bronchitis. His treatment was the same as that for angina sufferers. He had to gargle with the potassium permanganate solution. But Teras's condition continued to worsen. I ordered him to stop smoking, but he continued to misbehave in secret.

I asked Gleb Nikolajevich to admit Teras to a hospital. Two weeks later, the patient died – of tuberculosis.

New patients arrived at the inpatient clinic every day. Most of them were thieves who hoped to escape the transports by being ill. Their illnesses were fictitious, and their fevers artificially induced. Gleb Nikolajevich wanted to stay on good terms with them, and agreed to admit them.

My own work became more difficult, and yet much easier: more difficult under the critical gaze of my conscience, but easier in actuality.

Whenever I approached one of these men with my thermometer, he would say resolutely: "Write down 37.7 degrees" or "Write down 38 degrees." And I would do so. Gleb Nikolajevich had admitted them; I could not make them leave. Each one told me what disease he was suffering from. And when I offered them a swig of the potassium permanganate, all of them, one after another, told me to shove it up my ass. And everything was just fine.

The officials making the prisoner transport lists would often visit the inpatient clinic to see how things were going. By law, they were not allowed to place feverish persons in the transports. The malingering hypochondriacs kept convincing us of their need for continued idleness, a day at a time.

One morning, before Gleb Nikolajevich arrives for his office hours, one of our camp guards storms into the inpatient clinic with half a dozen stick-wielding men.

He bellows: "Everyone without a fever – get up!"

Nobody makes a sound.

I approach this enraged dictator of a guard and meekly show him the record of yesterday's fevers. He takes it from me. Since he is obviously an educated man, it only takes him a few seconds to realize what is going on. He throws the paper back at me disdainfully and bellows: "I'm the doctor here!"

That is the signal for the stick-wielding men. They raise their sticks and begin pummeling the hypochondriacs as well as the genuinely sick. Anyone failing to clamber down from his bunk fast enough is whacked across the back. Amid the confusion, a terrible howling swells from the bunks and the floor. The young Russians howl and squeal like animals. I crouch by the clinic door, hoping to make myself invisible, hoping to be spared this terrible beating. Cowering in the shadow of a bunk, I listen to the inhuman screams. They sound like shrieks of hopelessness emanating from all Creation. Cries for help fill the air, although I am sure that none of the men expect any help to arrive.

When all the well and the sick have been clubbed into a pile on the barrack floor, the barrack doors are opened, and the men are shoved out through a gauntlet of stick-wielding thugs.

The *sukas* recognize the faces of all the *urkas*[27]. Each one receives another whack before lining up. Mercifully, the *freiers*[28] are only threatened with a raised club. They need to be properly frightened, just for good measure.

And I am left alone in the barrack.

Gleb Nikolajevich does not come in that day. Even the duty officer has disappeared. Perhaps he himself was taken away in the confusion.

Now I gather up my meager belongings and walk meekly back to the barrack in which I had begun my medical career.

(Magadan Transit Camp, September 1948.)

27 *urkas* – Professional thieves who terrorize and rob other prisoners

28 *freiers* – Non-thieves; prisoners because of their political beliefs or faith

A THIEF'S WORD OF HONOR

"I give you my thief's word of honor that I'll return your needle."

"Today?"

"Fine, I'll bring it back after lunch."

After he has gone, things are rather quiet. I would never have imagined that even thieves have a word of honor, and never have believed that I might trust a thief's word of honor. Jurka is a thief. But when I lend him my needle, I cannot imagine him being a member of the thieves' guild. In my opinion, he is an unpretentious young man, who very politely asked to borrow my needle to sew two buttons onto his *fufaika*. But when he fails to return my needle that day and the next, I begin doubting his honesty. And now I see him heading for the inpatient clinic. I confront him: "My son, you borrowed my needle and promised to return it when you had finished sewing your buttons. You've been sewing your buttons for nearly a week, and I still haven't seen my needle."

"Did you give me a needle? I don't remember. You must be confusing me with someone else." He speaks so politely that I might almost believe that I am directing my suspicions at the wrong man for taking my needle.

But a Ukrainian engineer comes to my aid; he had also asked to borrow my needle. He knows the language of the camps much better than I, and refreshes the young man's memory right then and there. Cursing a blue streak, he swears to make mincemeat out of the brat if he does not return *batja*'s needle. That causes the polite young thief to hesitate. He quickly makes up a lie, saying he has lost the needle. My Ukrainian comrade becomes enraged. Shouting obscenities, he grabs the boy's shirt collar and swears he will smash him to bits right now. That works. Jurka makes up a new version of how he lost the needle. He lent it to another Russian, who probably lost it. As the Ukrainian begins to wring Jurka's shirt collar ever more tightly around his throat, Jurka gives a thief's word of honor. I ask my Ukrainian friend to free him. To expedite the return of my needle, I promise him half of my bread rations. He asks: "Why is this needle so important to you?"

"If you knew what I had to go through to make this needle and to hide this needle, you wouldn't be asking."

He did not ask me anything else, but stared at me for a long time with his intelligent gaze, in which only now I glimpsed the arrogance and cunning of a thief. He assured me once more, without having taken any offense at his brutal treatment: "*Batya*, don't worry, I give you my thief's word of honor that I'll bring your needle back."

If that gaze had not succeeded in misleading me at first, I would never have spoken to him again. I could not possibly trust a thief's word of honor. This man was able to lie so arrogantly without the smallest pang of conscience. But this thief's word of honor became something of a fragile anchor onto which I hitched my hopes of getting my needle back. And I realized that I had every right to be worried about the fate of my needle.

How had I come into the possession of my needle?

We were provided with a pleasant diversion one day in my cell at Patarei Prison. Electricians entered our cell to repair some damaged wiring. They left behind a quarter of a newspaper page and a small piece of copper wire. I found that piece of wire. It was the length of a decent darning needle. The thought of fashioning a needle came to me immediately. I showed my prize to a man I trusted; he had heard about bits of wire being made into needles before.

"But how can we make an eye for the needle?"

"By scraping it with a shard of glass," suggested my cellmate.

I now had a blueprint for fashioning my needle, but where would I get the shard of glass? With a spoon handle, I flattened one end of the wire against the iron bars on the window. That took nearly half a day. After that, I scraped the other end of the wire to make a needlepoint. That took another half a day. Then, to finish my needle, I had to find a shard of glass.

It was bath day once again. I was lucky: someone smashed one of the bathhouse door's tiny windows that allowed the guards to keep an eye on us. This caused an incredible uproar. Half a dozen guards stormed into the bathhouse room, all trying to ascertain the guilty party while picking up the pieces of glass. We were all standing there stark naked. That made it easy for the guards to search us. Each one of us had to open his hands to show the guards that no one had filched a piece of glass, which we might use to shave or to slit our wrists with. I did not have any glass in my hand. But I did have a sliver under my toe. And no one ordered us to lift our feet. With my foot, I cautiously pushed my treasure under a bench where nobody would think of looking for it. Finally convinced that none of their charges had picked up any glass from the bathhouse floor, the guards took their loot and left. Naturally, they did not use these pieces to reassemble the window, and simply threw them into the trash pit. Otherwise, they might have discovered that one piece was missing. Now it was mine. After I finished washing, I picked up some discarded slivers of soap. I smashed them together into a ball, hiding my treasure inside. Nobody stopped me from taking the soap back to the cell. The guard who searched me at the cell door probably thought I was a cultured individual who holds cleanliness in high esteem.

Excited, I continued making my needle. It was not only a test of my patience, but a thrilling adventure. All the time I was scratching the eye into my needle, I had to be talking to one of my friends, so that the cell's snitch would not notice what I was doing and betray me. If he did, I would not only be relieved of my needle, but would be placed in the cold isolation cell and left to regret my creative endeavors.

It took several days for my efforts to bear fruit. Finally, one morning, I could see light shining through the eye of my needle. I wanted to announce my success to the entire cell. But I could not, for the needle's sake as well as my own. The needle became my secret comrade, which I loaned out to only my most trusted friends.

Throughout all the searches on all the prisoner transports, the guards never noticed it. Even if one of them twisted and kneaded my lapels, the copper-wire needle remained undiscovered, since it would bend under the guard's fingers and never prick him.

And now I had given my needle to this young man who had probably traded it for a pinch of cheap tobacco. Naturally, he had no idea of what this needle meant to me. He could never comprehend the excitement that filled my days and my sleepless nights, when my only thought was of finishing this needle. To that young thief, the needle was nothing more than a piece of copper wire, a needle of dubious quality. Perhaps my concern about the needle had aroused a trace of sympathy in that thief, enough to bring forth that unusual promise, an oath that was hard to believe, and even harder to disbelieve: "I give you a thief's word of honor that I'll bring back your needle."

The day of his promise was approaching nighttime, but the young man was nowhere to be seen. I berated myself for my gullibility. It has caused me disappointment all too often. But I refused to lose hope. After all, Jurka was still a boy, and could not possibly be as depraved as the old recidivist Shulna.

If Shulna had given me his thief's word of honor, I would not have believed him for a moment. He would steal something right under my nose and deny it up to the moment all his pockets were turned inside out. And if the object was not found in his pockets, it would be found under a bunk. But if the item that he filched was never found, he would never return it, even if someone threatened to kill him over it. Nothing was sacred to him any more. He lived in the camps just as he had lived as a free man. Although his food rations in the transit camp were the same as all the other prisoners', he rarely ate it himself. He usually lost it gambling. Often, he would walk across the camp yard nearly naked in freezing weather, wearing only underpants. He had lost all his clothes gambling. When he got new ones, they would also be gone within two days. Again, he was left naked. But he lived on. He stole anything he could get his hands on. But even the quilted coat he had stolen did not cover him for long. The rightful owner had no chance of ever getting it back from him. Another thief, after winning the coat in a game, had already let some former thief and current transport guard trade it for a package of cheap tobacco or a swig of vodka. The thieves were on excellent terms with the speculators in town.

But Jurka could not possibly be such a thief.

Shulna would never claim that a thief has a word of honor. The thought of actually returning something would never occur to a true thief. Even promising to return something would represent an insult to the brotherhood of thieves. It would mean the awakening of a conscience. No, Jurka could not be that kind of thief. There had to be some remnants of human compassion still left in him. Perhaps he had a mother who prayed for him, who believed that Jurka would not be ruined for ever.

But he is not coming. He is not keeping his promise. The "thief's word of honor" does not exist. It is nothing but lies and deception. Dejectedly, I decide to erase the memory of the painstakingly fashioned needle from my heart.

But Jurka comes. Without a word, he takes my needle from under his *fufaika* and says: "I believe this is it."

"That's it!" I reply excitedly.

And suddenly, I deeply regret doubting this young thief's word of honor. I almost want to ask his forgiveness, to somehow make up for the insult he suffered when that Ukrainian giant twisted his collar. But I cannot find the words with which to approach Jurka. From my bunk, I take half my bread rations which I had put aside for him and give it to him, saying: "Thank you very much for keeping your word. You are, after all, a good boy. May God bless you. And here are half my bread rations, which I promised you."

But Jurka seems not to even notice my bread. He does not reach for it, because his gaze is drawn toward the door of the duty officer's room, which is slightly ajar. Without a word, he turns his back to me and briefly enters the duty officer's room before leaving the barrack. I had thought he was an old friend of the duty officer. But the duty officer is not there at the moment, and Jurka is in and out of his room less than ten seconds.

When the duty officer returned to the barrack, he immediately raised a ruckus. His entire ration had been stolen.

None of us had taken it.

Word of honor.

(Magadan Transit Camp, 1948.)

ABOUT THE COMPATRIOT IN THE WHITE COAT

After the thieves had turned it into their own private sanatorium, the camp stopped admitting the really sick to the inpatient clinic. We now had to visit a doctor in the work zone.

I decided to visit the dentist one day to tell him my problems. Scurvy was ravaging my body so cruelly that my teeth were just crumbling out of my gums.

There was a long line at the dentist's "office," but prisoners have lots of time. And when it comes time for the distribution of our food rations, they will not let us just sit around. The brigade commander must make sure that all his men are present to receive their rations. Therefore, I have nothing to worry about and nowhere to hurry. An old man with a pockmarked face sits next to me on the bench. I try talking with him to pass the time. He is not very talkative. Perhaps one of his horrible yellow fangs is so sore that it hurts him to open his mouth. However, he does tell me that the dentist is a very wise man. The dentist is not Russian, says my companio. He is not sure what the dentist's nationality might be. But he is good at what he does. Trying to sound knowledgeable, I remark: "No doubt they've assembled all kinds of specialists up here."

The pockmarked man simply grunts in reply.

I ask the old man how long he has been a prisoner.

He says: "I've been in this system for twenty-two years, and I no longer have any idea how I should wriggle my way out of it."

This is a very odd reply, and I must have stared at him rather stupidly, not knowing whether I should express sympathy or awe.

Politely, he returns my question: "And you, how long have you been imprisoned?"

Rather meekly, I reply: "I have lost my freedom just recently."

"And what did you do as a free man?" asks the old man.

"I was a cleric."

"Don't worry, *batyushka*, you'll do your time, and then you'll put your robe back on and start swinging your censer again," says the amiable recidivist, trying to console me.

We do not talk any more. Soon, a white-coated dentist appears at the threshold and calls out: "Next!" From that one spoken Russian word, I can tell that the dentist is Estonian. My compatriots have such a terrible accent when speaking Russian that I can tell their nationality from a single syllable of spoken Russian. My companion is the next to go in. I cannot figure out why he should be next, since there are five men sitting closer to the door than he. But he just stands up and goes in. Nobody protests. A few watch him with obligatory deference until he disappears into the dentist's office. Even after he is gone, nobody dares open his mouth. I think to myself – this old man must be someone important. Why else would he have been forced to live on a diet of prison bread for the last twenty-two years?

The dentist spends a long time treating the pockmarked man. We hear the whine of the drill, occasionally punctuated by a hoarse oath, no doubt marking the moments when he hurts the old fellow. When the pockmarked man, patting his cheek, finally leaves the office, the whitecoat does not immediately call in the next person. One man has already risen and is standing by the door, to make sure that nobody arbitrarily changes the admitting order again.

When the dentist appears at the threshold and casts an apologetic look over those left waiting, I mumble in Estonian: "I wonder if my turn will ever come today."

This introduction is enough for my countryman. He comes over to me, shakes my hand heartily, and without turning his attention to anyone else, invites me in. With total lack of reverence, the others begin to curse, but the doctor ignores them. He does not dignify the reaction of his patients with a single word of apology.

My dental treatment is quite simple. He examines my loose teeth knowledgeably and says: "Damn scurvy! There's nothing we can do about it. It won't be over until they've all fallen out of your mouth. But you do have a gold crown. You might as well use it to get yourself a swig of vodka. Otherwise, the guys at the barracks will yank it out of your mouth, tooth and all."

I feel my gold crown with my finger. It is far in the back, not particularly visible. I feel it firmly embedded in the gum. I have no particular desire to be relieved of it. I halfheartedly promise my compatriot that we will remove the crown for bartering purposes when the tooth becomes loose. That seems to satisfy him. And my dental treatment is done. We say heartfelt good-byes and once again, he calls from the door with his heavy Estonian accent: "Next!"

I never went back to him again. At inspection, I met some Estonians who knew him. One man claimed that out "dentist" had worked as a baker back in Tallinn. He was sure he had worked in a pastry factory with that "dentist," who had been a clever boy and an enterprising businessman. They had both been imprisoned on the same charges. And what do you know – the man is now a doctor! Later, I heard stories about the dental work he did for the officers. He visited the mortuary, removing gold crowns from the dead bodies (whatever was left after all the incursions by local robbers), and mounted the crowns onto the teeth of the officers and their wives. Many of them asked him to mount gold crowns on perfectly healthy teeth. I must give my compatriot credit for never melting the gold crowns down. They were transferred, already formed, from a dead man's mouth to a living man's or woman's mouth. These patients had to submit to a painstaking procedure if they wanted to show off some gold teeth.

I have no idea if this Estonian dentist ever managed to maintain his fine reputation. Perhaps he has continued a successful practice somewhere.

In the camps, there were other Estonian men equally as clever and enterprising. One of my valiant countrymen in the Canyon Labor Camp, Erik Kokka, cured all kinds of ailments and even assisted women giving birth in the free workers' settlement. He had been imprisoned in 1942 as a second lieutenant in the tank regiment. His specialty was auto mechanics. But his fame as a doctor was known far and wide throughout the region.

Another "doctor," Aleksander Kiima, had studied six semesters of law at the university in Estonia. However, he treated sick people so successfully in Lazo that he was given an official medical license upon his release. He managed to ruin his medical career by developing an excessive affinity for strong drink. His reputation as a doctor disintegrated rapidly. With much difficulty, his compatriots managed to stuff him into an airplane and send him away from Seimchan before he hit rock-bottom.

These days of misery have served as something of a filter, a purging process. Our small nation must not lose hope if this filtering has brought forth enterprising men and women such as the ones I met during this terrible time of trial.

My gold crown came out while I was at the Canyon Labor Camp. I kept it wrapped in a small rag for a long time, until regime commanger Lazos took it from me, without a word of thanks. No doubt he had one of his teeth filed down so that he might be able to prance around and show off the gold crown that had once belonged to me.

(Magadan Transit Camp, 1948.)

I PREDICT A MISERABLE FUTURE

I do not know why that Jew with the flattened nose was called Sasha. Usually, they are all called Lyova. He was one of the most vile creatures I ever encountered among the *suka* guards.

He was never without his club. I am sure he slept on his bunk with the club in his hand. At any camp he guarded, everyone knew it was wise to give this monster a wide berth. Sometimes he would sit in the cabinetmakers' workshop and boast about the murders he had committed. I suspect that he never actually committed them, but he bragged about it just the same. I suspect that the others in the gang did the actual killing and stealing, whereas he just egged the others on. He had hung around the camps for a number of years, and was soon to be released. Naturally, he was a one of the so-called "friends of the people," forced by circumstances into a life of crime. Basically, he was a loyal Soviet citizen. Ideologically he was truly without reproach. He boasted about having been accepted into the Communist Party without question because he had been a *Komsomol* secretary.

But this might just as well be a lie. Men like him were the pillars of the entire system. Naturally, they were entrusted with the most responsible duties, such as reining in the camp's "fascists."

And yet, it would be unfair to say that Sasha was a coward. His nose must have been smashed flat in a fight. In our transit camp, Sasha had indeed been a most enthusiastic participant in the rumbles between the *urkas* and *sukas*. With the help of his club, of course.

He was very resolute in his actions.

Barrack 6 was the place to enjoy all the pleasures the camp had to offer. It was there that they played cards, drank *chifir*[29], and bantered with each other.

One day, after leaving the mess tent, one pale boy refuses to return to Barrack 6. The duty officer yells at him, but the boy ignores it. I am watching from the cabinetmakers' workshop window.

Finally, the duty officer gets tired of wasting his breath and locks the barrack door. The boy, standing like a pillar of salt, is left outside to freeze. He is wearing only a field shirt. Outside, the temperature is frosty, about thirty below zero. I feel sorry for the boy. I go over to him and invite him into our hut for warmth. But the boy refuses to move. At my invitation, he merely hisses "F---ing sodomites!"

Apparently, the boy has been raped once too often. And now he has had enough.

And then, Sasha appears. Such disregard for the rules! Someone is just hanging around. Right away, Sasha implements his club. He whacks the boy across the back. But the boy only casts a pleading look at his tormentor and refuses to budge. The boy has character. That makes Sasha so angry that he begins to beat the boy without mercy. Blood pours from the young man's nose and ears. He falls to the matted snow. I think that Sasha is trying to beat the boy to death. I dart from the workshop, grab Sasha and scream: "You idiot, what are you doing?"

Suddenly, someone grabs my shoulder. A burly man is standing behind me. He says quite calmly: "*Batja*, don't bother him. He might kill you too. Go away. This doesn't concern you. This is the law of the camp."

And I leave. The law of the camp. The burly man is an old thief named Bykov, a man who relinquished his thief's mantle and is now a member of our camp's gang of *sukas*. And the *suka* guards stick together. The boy whom Sasha is beating to death is a mere prisoner. And I am not allowed to take the prisoners' side. I am a *freier,* a non-thief. I have no right to interfere in their affairs. A man is killed right before my eyes, and I may not say a single word in protest.

Shortly after, the boy's body is placed on a sled and removed from the camp.

---

29 *chifir* – Very, very potent fermented tea

Sasha walks around the zone with his club as if nothing has happened. Since that day, I can do nothing but despise that monster of a man whenever he crosses my path.

One day, he comes into our hut and asks me: "Haamer, do you speak German?"

"Yes, I do. Why?"

"Come with me!" orders Sasha.

I go.

He takes me to the inpatient clinic. My old acquaintance, Wehrmacht Hauptmann von Bassewitsch, is sitting on a bunk. He is an inpatient again. Back when I was there taking the temperature of the hypochondriacs, I was forever having to translate the nonsense that he told the Russian boys. He claimed to be a palm reader. He would take his client's hand, gaze at the palm searchingly, and start babbling: "You have experienced many adventures. Many of them have had significant impact on your life. At the age of twelve, you nearly lost your life in an accident. But all misery is temporary. Miraculously, you have escaped many misfortunes, and your misery will soon come to an end. You can expect great changes in your destiny. You will be released by next fall, at the latest. That is all that I can tell from your lines without a magnifying glass."

I have already memorized the nonsensical prattle used by this old German colonel to earn himself a piece of bread or half a herring. Nobody visits a palm reader without bringing a gift.

Sasha is as superstitious as all the other godless pickpockets. He wants me to translate what the palm reader can glean from the lines on his hand.

Fine, I will interpret. The old gray-haired officer takes the Jewish hooligan's hand into both of his, gazes attentively at the palm and starts the same old story: "You have experienced many adventures. Many of them have had significant impact on your life, etc., etc. ..."

I could have related that same story to Sasha without having to leave my bench at the cabinetmakers' workshop. But all right, he wants me to interpret everything exactly as it is told. When von Bassewitsch has finished, I ask: "Do you want only the good news, or the bad news too?"

"Everything!" answers Sasha resolutely.

And I begin: "The energy and character you exhibited in childhood were very promising. But now that promise has come to naught. You should have taken the things that have happened to you in your life as a warning to mend your ways. But you have ignored these warnings."

(I knew that Sasha was to be released in May.)

"You were scheduled for release when the flowers bloom in May. But now, because of your uncontrolled behavior, you have guaranteed postponement of your release. It will be postponed for a long time; it is hard to say how long. And if you continue behaving the way you have up to now, then you will be buried in the ground before the year is out. That is all that I can tell from your lines without a magnifying glass."

Sasha's ruddy face pales. Only his smashed nose keeps its color.

He says to me: "He has predicted bad things for me. Tell him I won't pay him shit for predictions like that."

I tell him: "I can understand if you don't pay me for interpreting. But you must pay him. You can be sure he did not lie to you. He read it all from your own palm."

"Ah, him and his f---ing mouth!" Sasha sighs and leaves.

"What? Wasn't he satisfied?" the palm-reading colonel asks, stunned.

"You know, sir, you could have predicted that he would soon receive the Medal of Stalin, and he would still not be satisfied, because these guys are crooks through and through. He cannot bring himself to give you a piece of bread or a cup of tea; that's why he's pretending to be dissatisfied."

My explanation satisfied Bassewitsch.

Sasha did indeed send him half a herring.

Two days before Christmas, the prediction came true as told. Sasha stormed into Barrack 6 to suppress a riot. They carried him out of there, barely alive.

Three days later, the brute's life came to an end in the transit camp's hospital.

(Magadan Transit Camp, November 1948.)

I WILL GIVE YOU A TORTE!

"Harri, guess what, today is my birthday!" I am given this information by a former officer in the German occupation force, a wry-faced young man who slept in the next bunk during the lengthy trip on the prisoner transport.

"I didn't know that, but now I know," I reply.

"How old are you?"

"Twenty-five."

"Well, that's a very important birthday. Best wishes!"

With a wretched smile, he holds out his hand and says: "Thanks!"

But I tease him by continuing on the topic of his birthday. "What would you like for a birthday present?"

"I would like nothing better than to get my fill to eat," says the birthday boy rather sadly.

It is midday, and the only food we can expect is a couple hundred grams of some thin flour-and-water mush.

"Have you eaten all your rations yet?"

"They're all gone," he replies with a wave of his hand.

"That was rather greedy of you," I chide him.

"I usually keep a bit of bread for the evening, but since today is my birthday, I gobbled all my rations at one time. I was hoping to eat my fill, just this once," the young man says plaintively.

I would not have been able to eat an entire ration of 800 grams of bread ration at one time. Perhaps an old man like me no longer needs to eat that much. But then again, I have seen men older than myself carefully gather up bowls left in the meal tent and sip the last remnants of soup from them.

I had occasionally been rather hungry when I lay in the inpatient clinic. I was very happy if someone left a little of their soup for me. Eventually, I learned to suppress my hunger pangs, especially when I listened to the other men constantly complaining of hunger.

Today, on my young friend's birthday, my rations are almost untouched.

Not knowing what words of comfort I should share with the birthday boy, I hurry back to my barrack. At that time, I lived in the underground workshop. It was a place where the camp's chief officers would have the artisans do all kinds of work off the books for the staff officers and the supervisors. We would repair their shoes and sew clothing, restore furniture and manufacture all kinds of objects, from sewing needles to cigarette lighters.

I had been recruited to this workshop as an artisan; I ended up carving wooden toys.

Occasionally, my work would be rewarded with an additional bowl of soup. However, my payment usually consisted of nothing more than the praise of the *pridurkas*[30], who thought I was a famous artist.

The day before, one of the *pridurkas* had rewarded me with some candy. He had given the camp guards an armful of toys I had made. They sold the toys at the market in Magadan. Apparently, they had shared their profits of their sale with the company commander, because he was pretty drunk when he placed the five candies in my hand. He took them from his pocket and presented them to me as if he were doing me a great favor, saying: "Here, take these, and don't think that I do not value your work."

"Thank you very much!" I told the patronizing wretch as I accepted the candies. He was not trying to insult me in any way. He gave the candies to me out of the goodness of his heart. In the circumstances we were in, it was indeed rare to meet a man who who still has a vague idea of what a conscience is.

I had kept those candies. They were wrapped in a tiny rag and tucked beneath the head of my bunk. Because the men in my workshop were all reasonably well fed, I was not afraid that they would steal the candies.

30 *pridurka* – A trusty, or political prisoner who sides with the regime for rank and other perks

There were only seven of us, and we could trust each other, since none of us were actual criminals.

And now, I can eat my bread rations and these candies in honor of Juhan's birthday. I take my bread from its hiding place on my bunk. I have already removed some crumbs, fastened to the loaf with wooden picks, to put in my soup. There are about 700 grams of bread left. I stick the candies into the bread, one at a time. It looks wonderful, just like a torte. Oh boy, if this was in Juhan's hands, he would just wolf it down.

My mind goes blank. My rations are suddenly burning my fingers. An inner voice tells me: "Take it to Juhan. It's his birthday, after all!"

I get down off my bunk, stuff my rations under my coat and go. I had kept two candies for myself. Angrily, I had eaten one right away, and the other I kept for later.

I find Juhan sitting on the edge of his bunk in the large barrack, lost in thought. With no fanfare, I hand him the rations, saying: "I brought you a birthday torte!"

What a shine brightens his face! "Yes, indeed, this is a real torte. Thank you so very much!" And he immediately begins to gobble it down. I stand next to him and feel very content at the happiness I have given this 25-year-old child. I have given him a whole kingdom from the folds of my quilted coat.

He has saved the last candy for his final treat. Before eating it, he looks at it with great tenderness, as if looking at an apparition or some treasure of tremendous value. Suddenly, his face turns serious and he looks at me in astonishment. He stutters: "But these are your rations." – "Of course they're mine; you can't possibly think I've stolen them. And now they belong to you. Remember that. And they're not rations. What you have is a torte."

"This is the best torte I have ever eaten, and will always be the best torte I have ever eaten," swears the young man at his birthday "banquet."

Indeed, he never forgot. Nine years later, when he was sent back to his homeland as an invalid, he came to look for me at my former home in Tartu. But I was no longer there. He met my children and told them the story of his birthday torte, which I had already long forgotten.

He, however, could not forget it.

(Magadan Transit Camp, November 1948)

THE COMMON LANGUAGE OF GOD'S CHILDREN

All the undemanding men have to sleep on the floor. The land in which a man may "breathe free" is large and vast, but the space in which a prisoner may lay his head is cramped and limited. A barrack with sleeping space for two hundred men must house five hundred. Even this space has been calculated to give each man a width of about 20 centimeters. In these conditions, it is impossible to curl up or to turn around. If your ribs ache from lying on a crack between the planks, you cannot turn the other side at your own discretion. You have to wait for the command of "Turn!" from one end of the bunks to rescue you. When they hear this, all two hundred men turn the other side. In mid-winter, conditions are so miserable that nobody can easily travel any distance from the transit camp. During the day, when most men are at work, you at least have enough space to sit on the edge of the bunks. But nobody will let you sit there at night. In Barrack 4, I had to stand upright for four nights in a row. I clung to a bunk post to avoid falling over from exhaustion. I longed for only one thing: to have just a sliver of a bunk to doze on briefly for at least one night. And when that night came, I wanted even more. Now I wanted the night to come when I could lie down on the floor. That night came. Even though the men making their way to the bunks in the rear would step right on your face, at least it was much better than standing on your feet all night, serenaded by the snoring of sleeping prisoners.

Not one man cared to relinquish his space to the six Japanese officers. They spent their days talking to each other, and their nights standing upright near me. They did not understand a word of Russian. I tried speaking to them in English. They shook their heads, smiling politely. Only one of them seemed to prick up his ears. But even he did not speak to me right away. Apparently, they were quite cautious.

One day, I am sitting on the edge of a bunk and reading my New Testament. One of the Japanese officers gets up, comes over to me, bows deeply and asks what is the book I am reading so intently.

"It is the New Testament," I reply without further explanation or comment.

"Oh, how I would love to hear that again," sighs the Japanese man.

"Are you a Christian?" I ask.

"Yes, I have been christened. My name is Stephen, but I used to be called Matsuo. And I attended an American Methodist Sunday School," my new friend explains.

I introduce myself and express joy at his interest in the Gospels. He asks: "Is your book in English?"

"No, it is in Estonian."

"Too bad, I do not understand any Estonian."

"But I can translate something for you," I offer. "What would you like me to read to you?" He brightens and asks me to read something about Stephen.

I begin translating the story of Stephen from Acts of the Apostles. Suddenly he stops me and asks if he may invite his friends to come and listen. They approach me with dignity, bow deeply and say something in their native language, smiling pleasantly. In my opinion, theirs is the world's most intelligent nation. Of all the representatives of the thirty-two nations that I have met in Soviet camps, the Japanese impress me as being the most cultured. Even the Germans lag far behind the Japanese.

These five men do not understand a word of English. Stephen, formerly Matsuo, interprets for them. Occasionally, they nod to indicate they are paying attention. Soon, I tire of struggling to express myself in a foreign language. Hoping for a break, I suggest that we sing something. Perhaps Stephen might remember a sacred song he learned in Sunday School. He starts singing a song that I know - "Rock of Ages." He sings only the first line in English. After that, he continues in Japanese. I sing along in Estonian. After we have sung a few verses, one of his companions says something in

Japanese. I ask him to interpret. Stephen says that his compatriot is surprised that Estonian sounds much the same as Japanese.

Stephen says something back to them. I ask him to interpret his response.

Stephen says: "I told them that the language of God's children is always one and the same."

What a wonderful testimony, a testimony given to me by a Japanese man, trying to evangelize his Shinto friends.

And yet, why must the languages of God's children so often be so different?

The next morning, the Japanese prisoners are taken away.

(Magadan Transit Camp, December 1948.)

THE HOLY NIGHT ON THE BARRACK FLOOR

"Harri, it's Christmas Eve!" one of my countrymen calls to me from the threshold of my hut as he returns to his own barrack from the mess tent.

"Come in and close the door!" snarls the engineer from Kuibyshev, who is our chief cabinetmaker and director of our workshop.

"Will we be celebrating Christmas?" my compatriot asks naively, standing by the door.

"Of course we will," I reply.

And we make plans for celebrating Christmas. The Estonians who have not yet been sent away with the transports are all in Barrack 4, except for me. I promise to take my book and go to them that evening.

The Russian Christmas is not for another thirteen days, so the Russians pay no attention to the fact that our cherished holy day has arrived. I had reminded my colleagues in the workshop of that several times. With the exception of a Lithuanian tinsmith, nobody paid attention. Just like every other day, we worked until dark.

Then, I brushed the workshop dust from my clothes, slid my New Testament into my pocket and headed for Barrack 4.

There were a couple dozen Estonian men left there. They all slept on the barrack floor, since the members of the nationality living in our neighboring country would always force their way onto the bunks.

As I entered, they were sitting on the floor, as usual, around the void left by a stove someone had torn out.

A newly built, poor excuse for a stove, thrown together by some self-styled potter, had begun spewing flames and smoke, and was removed from the barrack entirely. Now the room was heated only by the warmth of the bodies inside. When the outdoor thermometer read -40° C, it was comfortable enough to sit there in your quilted coat. But it was too cold to sleep, especially at floor level. For warmth, the men tried huddling very close together. And when the cold became unbearable, they got up and walked around to stay warm.

This is what happened to me in my own barrack. One night, I lay down on my bunk to sleep, my head by a window with a broken pane. Over time, the prisoners' breath had condensed in that space to form a thick block of ice. To keep the cold from this ice brick from flowing onto my head, I put an old Japanese soldier's hat on my head, tying it securely under my chin. When they woke us the following morning, I tried to get up, but my head was stuck to something. I had no choice but to untie the hat strings. The hat had frozen to the window while I slept.

We had no choice but to adapt. We were in a camp, and we had to acknowledge that these unforgiving conditions would be the venue for the re-education that was to mold us into good Soviet citizens.

The men make room for me right there on the floor. They had prepared a pulpit for me on Christmas Eve.

I begin my service by saying: "Today, Christmas begins."

The men are silent. Their expressions are serious and yet festive.

But the barrack resounds with a frightful din. Up on the bunks, men are playing cards, shouting, swearing. Four or five hundred men are making every possible kind of racket to ease their boredom. None of them gives a damn about the fact that twenty uprooted sons of Estonia wish to hear the joyous message of Christmas.

I cannot hear my own voice in the ruckus. I make a suggestion: "Men, my brothers, let's sing. Perhaps they will quiet down a little."

And we sing. Crouching on the floor, I start singing the lovely old carol "Silent night, holy night" in a loud voice. The men pick up my key and join me in song. We sing. We are the unfortunate children of our faraway homeland, singing here, in this cold and distant foreign land, where there is no room, no warmth, no peace for us. But we are singing to the One who was born as a Savior for the outcasts, the cold, the troubled. We sing, forgetting everything but the joy in knowing that tonight is a sacred night, Christmas Eve. We do not even notice that the uproar in the barrack is slowly subsiding, and soon everyone is listening to our song.

Silent night, holy night. This night is indeed silent and holy for us, the men who no longer have a homeland, who no longer have a home, who no longer have justice, who no longer have joy, but who still have hope.

When we finish singing, the barrack is strangely and solemnly quiet. If I read my Christmas gospel in a louder voice, even those in the farthest corner might be able to hear me. But my congregation is no larger than these twenty men here in the void of the wrecked stove. I give my Christmas sermon for them. We bow our heads to pray. I pray that Jesus, the Child of Christmas, will bless us this night with heavenly peace and solace, and bless those at home who are thinking of us with sorrow in their hearts. We give ourselves up to the grace of the Father, who has, even in these miserable conditions, given us joy through His Christmas Gospel and reassured us in this hopeless situation with the promise of eternal life.

When I say the Lord's Prayer, my voice is nearly a whisper, but not one word is lost. I get up and bid farewell to my brothers without singing the final hymn. I am afraid that our singing might disturb the solemn silence that has fallen over the barrack.

As I am walking out the door, a hand from the top bunk stops me. A smiling Russian boy looks at me with a sly face and says: "*Batya*, I know what you just did."

"And what might that be?"

"You held a service. It was beautiful."

He too has shared the occasion.

The duty officer who lets me out the barrack door asks: "What holiday are you celebrating?"

"Christmas," I reply.

(Magadan Transit Camp, December 24, 1948)

HOW I AM ANOINTED A THIEF

Only twenty minutes of fresh air. As if they were sorry to give the prisoners even that much. After a twenty-minute walk between the barracks, we have to climb back up on our bunks, once again in the stale barracks with the stench of farts and the toilet bucket. And when you run out of things to talk about, the melancholy overtakes you again. Your imagination takes you back to those you have left behind so far, far away. You know nothing about their lives. Perhaps they have met with some misfortune? Your heart becomes heavy. You ask – why have I been so cruelly punished? Were you really torn from your home, your country, your people, simply because you worked to instill Estonian youth with a simple middle-class patriotic spirit? Your entire life has been shattered. You might be separated from all that is dear to you for the eight years of your sentence, or perhaps for your whole life. And who is now preaching in your pulpit? Is there no one to protest against this injustice? Must you perish in this marked mass of humanity?

The more time you had to think, the more hopeless it all seemed. A mailman from Haapsalu had tried to comfort me in the basement of the Pagari Street KGB house with this advice: "There's no point to thinking in here." But I could not stop thinking. I felt my own devastation closing in on me, becoming more overwhelming every day.

During one of our "strolls," I looked up with envy on the men repairing the barrack roof. They were not herded back into the barracks when their twenty minutes in the fresh air are up. If only I could repair the roof along with them. A Jewish engineer from Ukraine was hurrying about next to the barracks. I had met him on the ship, where we had practiced English together. I went over and asked him if he could take me on as a roof worker.

"Have you done this kind of work before?"

"No, but I'll learn!"

"All right, we'll see," he replied.

The next morning, I was called out of the barrack without my belongings. That Ukrainian Jew had succeeded; I was to become a carpenter.

Excited, I climbed onto the roof, hammer in hand and nails cut from scrap sheet metal in my quilted coat pocket.

But I wanted to temper my joy in spending time in fresh air with useful pursuits. I truly wanted to become a carpenter. For that, I should receive carpenters' training.

Three men are already busy pounding on the roof. Whom should I begin working next to?

"Hey, are you a carpenter?" I ask the nearest man.

"No. Why should I have to be? I'm a ship's mechanic," he replies. I climb higher. A *fufaika*-clad figure is hammering shingles to the roof as if his life depends on it. "Hey, brother, are you a real carpenter?"

"No, I'm a baker."

Well, I probably will not learn much from him.

I climb even higher. An older man with an intelligent face is just reaching for a new shingle.

"Excuse me, are you a carpenter?"

"No, not yet. But maybe one day, I will be."

"So you didn't shingle roofs as a free man?"

"No, I was an agricultural scientist."

I do not need to doubt my abilities any longer. If all these men can work so diligently at hammering shingles onto the roof spars, without ever having done this work professionally, I suppose I will manage just as well.

I start working diligently, to stay warm. I have no idea how I am supposed to attach the shingles to the roof. But I follow the lead of the other "carpenters" before me. After all, I have hammered nails into wood before.

And I am praised for my work.

A few days later, the brigade commander presents me as an example to the others, who were just loafing, according to him.

Those were pleasant days. As payment, each man received an additional bowl of green soup, without lard. Some of the other guys had finished that off long ago.

But one day, there were no more shingles to hammer. For a while, we sat around idly. Since they could not find any other work for us to do, we were sent back behind the locked doors and barred windows of the barracks.

We were back in the same old staleness, the same din, the same discomfort, and the same melancholy thoughts. But the imprisonment only lasted for a few days.

They awaken the carpenters early one morning.

"Boys, get up quick!" It is our brigade commander. It is still dark outside. But we do not wait for him to ask twice. Immediately, we pull on our felt boots and wrap our quilted coats around us.

We are taken out to fetch shingles. The work zone gate is opened, but not a single red-epauletted guard comes with us. There are five of us plus the brigade commander. In the work zone yard, the snow is more heavily trampled down and grayer than ours. Apparently, the men here have somewhat more "freedom" to move about.

The brigade commander takes us to an enclosure, and points out the shingles, like a master to his servants. Each one of us grabs two bundles and leaves.

Prancing alongside, the brigade commander drives us on with: "Let's move it, boys!"

The men start to jog. Gradually, it dawns on me that we have just stolen something. In the dark yard, all I can see is a glowing cigarette, winking like a tiny red star. That must be the guard who has just been bribed with a pack of cheap tobacco. But I do not care. For me, this means that I can spend another whole day or more in the fresh air.

By the time we reach the sentry box, I can no longer keep step with my younger, better fed colleagues. The barracks are still 100-150 meters away. I put my shingle bundles down right there by the fence behind the sentry box, and sit down on them for a moment to catch my breath.

But the men are already running, breathless, back toward the sentry box. Seeing me, the brigade commander calls agitatedly: "Haamer, what happened to you? We're going back again. Come on, boys, let's run. I'll feed you..." Jogging briskly, we set out on another expedition.

We find only a few shingles left under that ragged roof of the enclosure. Each man can hoist only one bundle onto his back. Zealously, I gather up a large bunch of unpackaged shingles left from a bundle that had fallen apart. And I jog after the others. The faintest hint of dawn is beginning to glow.

We have not yet reached our camp gates when we see someone chasing us and shouting: "Stop, stop!" embellished with all the usual "f---s" and other oaths.

But I obey nobody but my own brigade commander. I have not the slightest concern for that angry voice coming up behind us, trying to reach us, wanting to catch up with the criminals. My feet move faster and faster. My lungs ache for breath. I am afraid I will fall behind my colleagues. I toss my burden against the fence behind the sentry box and slump onto the pile of shingles, panting.

An angry, bespectacled man wearing a Moscow coat rushes through the gate, past the sentry box into the camp as fast as his feet can carry him, chasing the shingle bearers. He races by me so fast that he does not even see me.

Having caught my breath, I hide my shingle bundles a little farther behind the sentry box and stumble back toward the barracks, where the air is thick with oaths and curses.

The angry man who had discovered our shingle acquisition enterprise turned out to be the manager of the work zone collective. I do not know if he was a free man or an outside professional working at the camp. The camps included plenty of both. Apparently, he had the arbitrary right to curse at anyone, even the manager of our own camp collective, Pjotr Maximovich Gerasimov. Gerasimov, a major from Marshal Rokossovski's army, was a genuine crook serving a 25-year sentence. He talked of his escapades in the Great Patriotic War, which had nothing to do with war, but rather involved robberies and murders committed behind the front lines. I do not know if he was awarded any medals for his activities before being tossed in jail. But now, Pjotr Maximovich remained meekly quiet, although he was wearing nearly the same kind of coat as the other official, a light overcoat known as a "Moscow coat."

A torrent of curses, like an unrelenting hail, clattered onto the head of our poor unfortunate brigade commander. "Son of a bitch, who taught you to steal?" the manager of the work zone collective shrieked, to which our own collective manager merely mumbled "F--- your mouth" three times in reply. That was one of his milder expressions. This whole thing had probably been his idea.

I began feeling sorry for the brigade commander. He was cowering so pitifully. Only now did I see the real Jew in him. I wanted to intervene on his behalf with a blunt and concise reply to that angry bespectacled man: "The only one that has taught us to steal is the Soviet system!" But I was already serving time for anti-Soviet propaganda, and I did not want to give them cause to impose a sentence any harsher than it already was. I watched in dull silence, picking up a few heretofore unknown Russian obscenities in the process. Our verdict was handed down right then and there. We had to carry the stolen shingles back to where we got them. However, the guard did not have to return the tobacco he had received in exchange for turning a blind eye to our activities.

Each of us had to hoist the two bundles of shingles onto his back once more and return them to their original location. A few men, curious passers-by who came to see what all the shouting was about, were recruited to help.

After we had returned our load to its original spot, the manager of the work zone collective, still enraged, escorted us back to the sentry box. As I was eager to enrich my vocabulary of Russian obscenities, I was the last to step through the gate. In honor of all us hoodlums, he gave me, as the last to enter, a swift kick in the buttocks. It did not hurt, but it was insulting, because I was sure I did not deserve it. However, the laws of the camps are like the laws of life in general. The little guy is the one who suffers.

The gate clanged shut and was bolted. Without a word, the men dispersed throughout the camp.

But my shingles still lay there behind the sentry box. I had nearly forgotten about them, and was prepared to calmly follow the others back into the camp. But the shingles entered my field of vision like an apparition in the gray snowdrift. What should I do? I felt my conscience stirring. An inner voice said: "These shingles were stolen too. Shouldn't you take them back?" But another voice countered: "Your reward for carrying them was a kick in the behind. They belong to you now. You have not stolen them; they have been left to you. The gate has been bolted, and the angry man has no idea how many shingles he is supposed to have. After all, you did not steal them for yourself."

I order my comrade conscience to get back to the barrack and take a whiff of the odor wafting from our toilet bucket. I heave the shingle bundles onto my shoulders and take them over to the barrack, with the roof that is so sorely in need of repair. Without further ado, I climb onto the roof and get to work. I take great pleasure in fitting shingle against shingle up there in the biting cold all by myself. I almost feel like whistling.

Suddenly, someone shouts from below: "Haamer, what are you doing?"

"I'm chopping wood!" I shout back.

"Get right down here!" orders my brigade commander, who seems to have recovered from the morning's commotion.

I climb down off the roof. The closer I get to earth, the more apprehensive I become. Now they will certainly lock me up in the dark solitary cell. I should have listened to my conscience and returned the shingles.

"Follow me!" The brigade commander barks his order in such an authoritative tone that I no longer doubt that a miserable destiny awaits me. What a terrible fate to be thrown into the *buri*[31]! They will take away my quilted coat. I will be forced to walk from corner to corner, day and night. The *buri* has no covers on the windows. I once saw a poor man shivering there in his shirtsleeves, begging for a cigarette through the window. Oh, how stupid I am! Once again, I have forgotten that I have not been brought to a vacation resort.

But the brigade commander makes his way to the mess tent. Is he giving me a bit to eat before I am forced to fast in solitary confinement?

We are truly in the mess tent. The cook is clattering his pots and bowls. We stop at the food distribution table. What will happen now?

"Hey, cook, you f--ing mouth, do you have any leftovers?" the brigade commander asks his old friend.

"We have some porridge."

"Give this man some," says the brigade commander, gesturing toward me and adding: "He deserves it."

I once darned this cook's torn socks, and he has not forgotten the favor.

---

31 *buri* – Isolation cell; unheated and with open windows; rations were bread and water

"I know this Estonian," says the cook without removing the cigarette butt from his mouth. He plops some barley porridge into a bowl, adds a small ladleful of seal blubber, slaps the bowl onto the counter with a professional gesture and shoves it toward me saying: "Enjoy this in good health."

"This is for me?" I stutter, dumbfounded.

"Of course it's for you, idiot," replies the cook.

"Well then, thank you, brother. May God reward you for your kindness," I stammer. I take off my hat, cross myself and praise God aloud in my native language before I begin to devour that bowl of porridge. But that is not the last of it. The brigade commander asks the cook if there is any tea left. The cook dips a ladleful of tea from a barrel. Most of the sugar designated for the prisoners has been filched, and yet the tea has a bit of sweetness which tastes just fine. And he shoves this toward me as well. Now my eyes brim with tears.

"Lord, how you have blessed me. I am getting my fill to eat, and I can eat all of it undisturbed. No club-wielding men will chase me out of here. Good Father, I am not worthy of such grace." I am truly moved, my heart is full of gratitude.

Suddenly, I realize – I am being rewarded for getting away with theft.

This means I am now an anointed thief. One bowl of porridge and another of tea represents the festive meal for this day of anointment. And now, if those thieves in Cell 17 should ever question me again, I can proudly state, without batting an eye: "I am a thief."

(This happened in the Magadan Transit Camp in March of 1949.)

MY REAR END IS TOO SKINNY

"It looks like they'll be checking our rear ends again," grumbles Captain Annuk as we are taken for our morning lineup.

If this had been the regular checkup, the entire camp complex would have been reverberating with shouts and screams. Barrack by barrack, the men are being taken over to the duty officer's window. A table has been set up in the sunshine at one end of the barrack, and several officers are sitting there. A group of well-fed gentlemen, some in uniforms, some in civilian clothes, bustle around them. I recognize the characteristics of the "chosen people" in many of the faces; fleshy hooked noses and pouty flaccid lower lips.

As soon as we have been lined up for inspection, the procedure commences without further ado.

"Pull your pants down!" orders a gold-epauletted man. We unbutton our pants, staring speechlessly at all these functionaries. The pot-bellied communists come up behind our backs and get to work. This job requires neither a doctor nor an expert. Each one of the functionaries judges us at his own discretion by the little bit of flesh left on our buttocks.

One pudgy man pulls the skin of my buttocks away from the bone with his fingers. He does not look in my face; he does not ask me who I am, what I have studied, what I am thinking, what I am suffering, what I am capable of. Nothing at all. This man is a specialist in this particular field only. His pinch finds not one bit of meat on my buttocks. Thanks to his extensive experience, he can base his decision on my potential usefulness or uselessness as a member of the workforce of the establishment that he leads on one pinch of my rear end.

"Unfit!" says each official, slapping each man's dystrophic buttocks with a disparaging whack. My esteemed expert pronounces the same assessment, but neglects to slap me. Perhaps he is afraid of hurting his fingers if he should hit them against the hipbones protruding through my skin.

And so, I am not called to the table to sign my name. Once again, I have been shown mercy.

As I pull my pants up again, I try hard to recall how long ago Harriet Beecher Stowe wrote "Uncle Tom's Cabin."

At that time, the situation in the United States must have been similar to that in the current Soviet Union. Black men with bare buttocks could be found only at slave markets. The men deciding their fate were hardly any different from these Soviet slave dealers.

But does anyone dare write about what is happening here? Will anyone ever dare publish a book about it?

Anyone who tries will meet the same fate soon enough.

But perhaps at some later time? Oh well, many years from now it will be of no use anymore.

Lenin once said: "...a slave who is aware of his status as a slave, and rebels against it, is a revolutionary." However, the people who are building up the system based on this man's ideas do not want their slaves to ever become aware of their status; they want slaves to remain slaves. Lenin had a few words for that situation too: "...a slave who does not know he is a slave, and who suffers his slavery silently, unwittingly and mutely, is simply a slave."

You see, that is exactly what they want from us. They want us to be simple, silent slaves. And those men executing "the rule of the proletariat" stroll behind us with the demeanor of a slavemaster, and decide our fate with the simplest of actions – a brief pinch of our buttocks.

(Magadan Transit Camp, May 1949.)

UPBRINGING AND EDUCATION HAVE FAILED

Jevgeni Vassilyevich had been a chemistry professor. I met him for the first time during a head count in Barrack 6. After that, we ended up living together for a few weeks. He was a truly well-educated man, six or seven years older that I, with an impeccable upbringing.

In the mornings, we greeted each other cordially, asked how the other was doing, expressed our feelings about sleeping on our hard resting place and wondered about the weather forecast for that day.

We passed our days in scientific discussion. We philosophized a great deal. Jevgeni Vassilyevich considered me to be an interesting conversationalist, and felt that our conversations broadened his perspective. He called our discussions a "course." In turn, I dedicated myself to learning the secrets of plastics manufacturing.

We barely noticed our dreary days rolling by.

There was only one topic we could not touch upon in our discussions – religion. Jevgeni Vassilyevich was an atheist, a staunch atheist.

Each time I broached the topic of God, he would give a twisted smile and suggest, without being insulting, that there was no need to bring up religious topics at all. However, one time he asked: "Tell me, Harri Aleksandrovich, why do you, an educated, well-bred man, need to believe in a God whose existence has been disproved by science?"

Without arguing against the scientific approach, I responded with childlike simplicity: "I am afraid, Jevgeni Vassilyevich. The misery we have endured has severely drained our human stamina. If our situation should worsen, I am afraid that I could not survive without God."

"Oh, don't worry, Harri Aleksandrovich, our education and upbringing will keep our heads above water. I promise you that. Believe me, that's the way it will be."

I was silent. But I was sure of one thing: If I should face even more horrible ordeals in the future, I doubted that simple education and upbringing could preserve my human dignity and maintain the purity of my embattled spirit.

Then, one morning, Jevgeni Vassilyevich was taken away to the transports. I, the dystrophic, was left in the transit camp for several more months to await transport.

Every night as I knelt before my bunk, I prayed that God would let me meet Jevgeni Vassilyevich once more in my lifetime.

And then, one day, my semi-idle existence at the transit camp came to an end. I was my turn to be transported.

The last 24 men of that prisoners' contingent were ordered to leave behind everything except what they were wearing and assemble at the sentry box. I placed my belongings and my blanket on the bunk, and left.

They loaded us into a truck at the camp gate. It was a short ride that ended at the Magadan airfield.

We were forced past a gauntlet of automatic-weapon wielding soldiers into a green transport plane. We began our journey into the unknown. We were not allowed to look out the airplane windows. Sitting on the floor, I was tall enough to peer out the window and see the snowy mountain peaks over which the "Douglas" aircraft was taking us.

After two hours, we landed at an airfield.

It was the end of May. The sun sparkled and birds sang. Once again, we were loaded into trucks and driven somewhere into the mountains on roads carved by water, making our progress laborious.

After being bumped around in a truck for a couple hundred kilometers, we arrived on the evening of the following day at a cobalt mine in need of fresh manpower.

The canyon, the camp, the settlement, the mine and the factory were all located in a long valley between two mountain ranges. A strong, drafty wind blew incessantly.

After working for a week in the construction brigade of this forced labor camp, I was suddenly transferred to the factory.

The thieving brigade commander, his eye on my chrome-leather boots, gave me a relatively comfortable job. I had to push a small tram of concentrated liquid cobalt from the factory to the dryer.

It is always interesting for a newcomer to explore a new place. While they shoveled my load onto the drying grates, I looked around the dryer. The entire dingy room was filled with stinking chemical vapors. A fire burned in several ovens tended by a sooty old man.

The ovens had been dug into the side of the mountain. The mouths of the ovens were a good distance beneath the grates from which I observed the scene.

I was just getting ready to return to my tram when the "stoker" climbs up from his ovens. His face brimming with joy, he calls out: "F--ing mouth, Harri Aleksandrovich!"

"Jevgeni Vassilyevich, it's you!" I reply, stunned. His job of stoking the ovens is not what surprised me; obviously, he had been assigned to the job because of his profession. He was working around the chemical vapors that had always excited him so much. I was stunned because of the obscenity. This was the first I had heard it from the mouth of a man I least expected it from.

"Jevgeni Vassilyevich, what has happened to you?" I inquire, not hiding my amazement.

"Me? Oh, I've become a true resident of the camps," he replies with feigned arrogance.

"But what happened to your education and upbringing, which were supposed to keep your head above water?"

"Those went the way of all flesh, just like everything else around here, back to your f--ing mother," he explains simply.

"Didn't I tell you that I was afraid to leave myself to the mercy of education and upbringing in such miserable conditions, when all my own strength in inadequate? Remember when you asked me why I believe in God? Now I can answer you. He has not deserted me. I lived among thieves for seven months, and none of their influence has rubbed off on me. I have not lost my human dignity or my hope to once again fulfill my high calling as a real human being. I have not been disappointed by my unending faith in God."

"But why, in this place, do you need any of that any more?" My old friend is agitatedly defending his decline.

"Why do you need human dignity here?" he continues. "You're dressed in rags, starving, scorned, homeless, stripped of all your rights and all hope. Ultimately, you're going to end up somewhere among those rocks." As he says that, he points to the camp cemetery which is visible across the river on the opposite slope.

"How can that be? We have enough clothes on our backs to keep out the cold wind," I counter. Naturally, I am not exactly wearing a fancy outfit. At the Magadan bathhouse, I had been given a short quilted coat and a shirt that didn't even cover my abdomen. But for half my bread rations, I had bought an old towel from the bathhouse attendant which I washed and sewed to the bottom of my shirt as an extension. Whenever I changed shirts at the bathhouse, my "extension" would still be there, and my abdomen stayed well protected from any drafts. "We are given enough to eat, enabling us to walk to the mines on our own two feet. It is not necessarily true that we are scorned, because we can refuse to listen to those *Komsomol* brats when they curse us. And stripped of hope? Never. We will not end up among those rocks. We will end up in heaven."

Up to this point, Jevgeni Vassilyevich has listened rather calmly. But now he stares at me blankly and repeats: "In heaven!" Perhaps he mumbles something else to himself that I do not hear. Suddenly, he covers his eyes with both hands and leans against the dryer gate. Large tears trickle between his grimy fingers onto the back of his hands.

"Jevgeni Vassilyevich, what's wrong?" I ask, confused.

"I envy you religious people!" he hisses angrily through his teeth, as if in hatred against the one who has hurt him.

And I stand tall in my rags, a starving and scorned man, homeless and stripped of rights, but not stripped of hope.

"Oh God, God, I have something left for others to envy. Be gracious unto me, so that I may never lose this enviable faith. Promise me that I will keep it in any situation, even if it should be a thousand times worse than this."

And in this land without hope, God heard my prayer.

(Written on Nov. 5, 1963 from my recollections. This incident happened in early June 1949 at the Canyon Labor Camp in Kolyma.)

FOR YOUR KIND HEART

"Your kind heart is really going to get you in trouble, brother," said Aava Riks one day as I shared my soup with a boy from Narva who lived in my barrack and suffered horribly from constant hunger. It never would have occurred to me to share my soup with him if he had not distracted me from the joy I was taking in my new spoon. I have no idea how I got a hold of it, but as soon as I brought it to my mouth, a glimmer of light reflected into my eyes. As I brought it to my mouth again, I caught an even more wonderful glint. That glimmer gave me so much joy that I forgot to finish my soup. I felt that God was trying to comfort me through this spoon, and that made me very happy. Suddenly, I noticed two hungry eyes staring at my soup bowl. I had seen this boy from Narva drain his soup bowl in a few gulps and wolf down the two green cabbage leaves he retrieved with his fingers. Now, he is probably thinking that I do not like my soup. Why else would I be dallying like this? He is waiting for me to leave. I am just starting to eat again when I notice the sad look in the young man's eyes. I can no longer be happy next to this hungry boy. I want to cheer him up. I ask: "My son, are you very hungry?"

"Yes, I am," he replies, swallowing.

"Well, go ahead and finish this soup!" With that, I push my soup bowl over to the boy. The boy does not wait for me to ask twice. He grabs my soup and guzzles it down. He digs out a cabbage leaf stuck in a groove of the bowl and pops it into his mouth, enjoying every bite. My joy returns when I see his satisfied, happy face. But when Aava Riks sees this, he warns me about being kindhearted. The next day, the boy slides in next to me in the mess tent. This time I also give him half my soup. He does not refuse.

Now I am suffering because of my kind heart. I have been assigned to the brigade of the Ossetian schoolteacher Zungayev. He is a greedy fellow and a devout Muslim. He is close with the camp's *pridurkas*, and quick to bark orders at anyone beneath him. He makes arbitrary decisions about how much bread each prisoner should receive. If you protest his decisions, you are sent underground to work with some very undesirable brigade. Therefore, all the brigade's members keep their mouths shut even when the injustice is glaringly evident.

At first, he left me in peace, thinking I could be useful to him. He saw the carvings that I made in my free time. He had me carve mountains, the moon and a bear onto his cigarette case. But even that did not stop him from developing a grudge.

They were distributing tobacco in the camp for the first time. Each man was given a pack of cheap *makhorka*[32] tobacco. They promised to give us some every ten days. Tobacco was a commodity in short supply. The residents of the free workers' village would give bread and even sugar to the prisoners working there, but never tobacco. Some unescorted prisoners from the gold mines, hungry for tobacco, had gone to the village, offering 15 grams of gold for a pack of tobacco. But nobody had sold it to them. There may have been even more tobacco at the camp; the men received home-grown stuff as well as quality tobacco in the packages they got from home. Some poor unfortunates even traded their bread for tobacco. In our brigade, an old man named Kala managed to commit this very crime against himself. He bartered his entire bread ration for a little bit of tobacco. He became so thin that we could hardly stand to look at him.

When the brigade commander gave me my pack of tobacco, he said: "You don't smoke, so why don't you let me have this?"

But I did not give it to the camp's brigade commander. I had a better idea. I called Kala over and asked him: "Do you want my tobacco?"

The man's eyes lit up. "But what do you want for it?"

"Indeed, what do I want for it? I won't give it to you for nothing. I will give it to you on one condition. If you start eating all your bread rations yourself, you can have my tobacco every time I get some. If I see you

---

32 *makhorka* – Cheap tobacco

exchanging one single mouthful of bread for tobacco, I will throw my pack of tobacco into the river right in front of your eyes. But I won't be giving it to the brigade commander to speculate with."

After listening patiently to my sermon, he asked: "What do I have to do now?"

"Do you believe in God?"

"Yes, I do."

"Well, then promise me in God's name that you won't exchange one single gram of bread for tobacco."

Kala became very solemn and gave me his word. I gave him my tobacco.

Two days later, a new ten-day cycle began. Our team gathered moss from the tundra within the borders of the work zone for insulating the cracks between the boards of the building being built by the machine shop. I liked that job, and I gathered the moss diligently. The other men took frequent smoke breaks as I continued gathering moss.

The team elder said "You're a little fool, *batya*, for working so hard. That Ossetian will never thank you for it." But I ignored him. They rolled their smokes behind the pile of moss; I roamed about the tundra.

And then I found a cranberry. This was in May. It was in a spot that had been walked across hundreds of times. But one red berry had been left for me. For me, it was almost a revelation. My heart filled with such emotion that I knelt right there and started to thank God out loud in my native language. I saw it as a special act of grace from the Heavenly Father, sent to bring me joy. I recalled the time I had gone cranberry-picking with my wife in Parika Bog. As we gathered them by the handful into our baskets, my heart had not been filled with as much excitement as it was now upon finding this single cranberry on this stretch of tundra bounded by barbed wire. The experience was so powerful that I wanted to save this red berry as a souvenir. But that would never have worked, so I decided to eat it. It tasted like the finest delicacy, reminiscent of the sweetest dessert. Never before and never after that have I ever popped such a sweet-tasting berry into my mouth. When I returned to the group with my load of moss, an old Lithuanian forest warden said, in his broken Russian: "Good job! *Batja* is in an excellent mood."

They finally got up and dragged themselves back to work. The day was long, and I scraped many more loads of moss from the tundra, but I did not find any more berries. Finding a solitary red berry would impress the memory of God's solace deeply into my heart; that is how it had to be. It is indeed wonderful that we can experience the grace of God in even the most insignificant event in our lives, such as coming across a single cranberry.

The next morning, as I received my rations, I was given only 500 grams of bread through the bread hatch. Before assembling at the gate, I rushed to see the overseer. He looked up my work orders. The brigade commander had assigned me only 25% of my usual rations. He was taking revenge for the tobacco I had given to Kala.

Perhaps Aava Riks was right.

But that Ossetian will most certainly not succeed in extorting my pack of *makhorka* for himself.

(Canyon Labor Camp, in the summer of 1949.)

IT IS SUNDAY IN MY HEART

The wind howled around the barracks all night. Once, it swelled into such a stormy gust that it tore away the corner of our barrack's tarpaulin roof and rolled it halfway off. From my place on the uppermost bunk, I could see the stars twinkling above me.

That blustery night was followed by a still, sunny summer morning.

Again, they are cursing and berating that poor pock-marked monk at the camp gate. That means it must be Sunday. He refuses to work on Sunday. He would rather be incarcerated in the isolation cell with only bread and water than violate the commandment about the Day of Rest.

Once, Nikolai Vyssokinski had seen me sitting by the barrack with my New Testament, and immediately came over to introduce himself and to become my friend. We had not yet discussed the issue of working on Sunday. Although he was a Catholic, he did not regard me as a heretic. Actually, he listened gladly to my interpretations of the Gospels and was glad to acquire a better understanding of piety. He was a member of the sorters' brigade, which was always led out the gate just before our brigade.

I had never made an issue out of working or not working on Sunday. One of my compatriots had once teased me by asking how the pastor was keeping the commandment regarding the observation of the Sabbath. Remorselessly, I responded: "There are no Sundays in hell."

But now, the Sabbath was making me restless. Nikolai Vyssokinski remains a slave of God, in spite of his circumstances. He is obeying the Lord's commandment the best way he can in these circumstances. But I am walking serenely out the camp gates to work at the sawmill.

As they count us out the gates by fives, old Ostapenko, the construction workshop's technical overseer, holds me tightly by the arm. That pleasant-faced Ukrainian bookkeeper, who has managed to grow himself a pot belly while living in the camp, is a great admirer of the Estonian language. There are several other men besides me in the construction workshop, and each of us are experts in our field. They are skilled, hard workers. Most important, they do not complain or whine like many of the other prisoners, members of other nationalities.

I have been a member of this brigade for only a few days. I was sent back here from the factory, where I fared relatively well for a regrettably short time, because I had refused to relinquish my chrome-leather boots to the brigade commander.

Back when I started working in the cabinetmakers' and sawmill brigade, old Ostapenko ignored me, thinking I was nothing special. I received no packages from home, and nobody gave me any special assignments. But now, he noticed that all my compatriots in the camp were looking up to me as their spiritual father, and that everyone else was starting to notice it too. Now, this Ukrainian busybody developed a bit more respect for me.

In the lineup, he starts showing off his Estonian vocabulary, which Heina Ruudi, the diminutive village carpenter from Viru County, had taught him. As the line starts to move, the bloodhounds start baying. "*Deeamn doggies!*" whispers Ostapenko, his face aglow at being able to express his feelings to me in my native language. We have marched only several dozen meters when thousands of mosquitoes attack us. They escort our line like a buzzing cloud that envelops our heads. "*Deeamn misskiitwoes!*" complains Ostapenko.

I have had enough. I reply to him in a low whisper, since we are forbidden to speak in line: "That's not Estonian."

"How's that?" Ostapenko is surprised.

"That's the language of the deeamned. And today is Sunday. Today, I don't want to hear that kind of language."

Ostapenko shuts up. And I begin preparing a sermon. For myself and for my people. A sermon that I may never be able to give in a clear voice from any pulpit on earth.

There are people, a regal people, consecrated for the sacred priesthood, set aside from the world for God. Why should such people be forced to deal with the foul language, the ideas, the beliefs you are surrounded by every day in a place like this? Why do you need to suffer in an environment that tries to instill those beliefs into you? What do you have in common with this low, vulgar and ridiculous gaggle of human beings with whom you walk a common path from the camp to the mines and back again? You have an entirely different calling. You would like to be with a completely different group of people, you would like to hear speech that is completely different from that which surrounds you here. But now you must walk among this throng in which nobody affirms you in your higher calling, and where nobody inspires you to fight for the privilege to be a member of the special group of people that God has set aside to serve Him.

In that whole camp, there is probably only one man who dares give public witness. It is that pockmarked monk who has been thrown into the isolation cell for refusing to work on a Sunday.

I say to myself: "You were ashamed of your nationality for no good reason that time in the Magadan Transit Camp when the Ukrainian medical attendant called the Estonians 'those damned people.' You are no better than 'those damned people,' even if you do not curse. Have you nothing to teach anyone, even to this self-satisfied camp trusty who is walking next to you and showing off his language skills?"

I am filled with sadness for the Sunday that I have lost. But not just for the Sunday. Is not my whole life being wasted in this hell, where there are not only no Sundays, but no people who deserve to celebrate a Sunday?

On this bright summer day, I walk down this path in the taiga[33], this kilometer trod flat by the footsteps of prisoners. And this day could be a Sunday. "Oh God, could this day still be a Sunday for me, in spite of everything that surrounds me here?" I sigh from deep within my heart, trying to find my way to the throne as a child of the Sabbath.

Soon we reach the bridge, and we are counted through the gates into the mines.

---

33 *taiga* – A vast coniferous forest in the far north

At the bridge, the dogs and automatic weapon-wielding *Komsomol* members turn back. Only the mosquitoes escort us down the slope into the mine.

Ostapenko no longer walks with me. Quietly, I plod up the soggy slope, and a wondrous calm envelops my heart. Somewhere, Sabbath bells begin ringing, and I feel them pealing their way into my soul.

"It is Sunday in my heart, filled with quiet joy and peace." Our choir used to sing those words. A thousand people listened. But I am afraid that their hearts did not experience the Sunday which I am experiencing this morning and all this day, as I mop the sweat from my brow.

When Brother Nikolai was released from the isolation cell, he sought me out right away. His first question was: "Tell me, how can you be so calm as you go to work on a Sunday?"

I motioned him to sit on the bench next to me and asked in turn: "What did you do this Sunday in the isolation cell?"

"I felt sad," was the unexpected reply.

"So – that means you didn't celebrate the Sabbath in a right and proper way," I chided my friend, the monk. "At first, I felt sad too, but then I remembered a beautiful song that begins with the words 'It is Sunday in my heart,' and my heart was immediately filled with the blessings of the Sabbath. In Russian, Sunday is *voskersenie (also translatable as "Resurrection").* You know what that reminds us of, as Christians. And why shouldn't you, with a heart that has experienced the Resurrection, unload rocks from a conveyor belt rather than pace the floor of an isolation cell?

There are no Sundays in hell, but even in hell, our hearts can experience Sunday, if they are filled with the blessings of the Resurrection."

Nikolai was silent for quite some time. Then he said: "Next Sunday, I will go to work. But I want to walk with you."

And so he did. The guards stood wide-eyed when Nikolai Vyssokinski prepared to exit the camp gates without a fight. Some of them nudged him approvingly. During a brief commotion by the camp gates, he slipped in next to me, although he was assigned to march with the sorters in the last row, while I was in one of the first rows of the construction brigade.

Ostapenko quietly took the monk's place when I indicated with a wink that he should do so. I would not have let him show off his fluency in the *deeamned* people's language anyway.

The day was cloudy and drizzly. At least it kept the mosquitoes from bothering us.

Nikolai clings tightly to my arm and whispers: "*Voskersenie, voskersenie*!"

And so we share the Sunday that has embedded itself in our hearts.

(Canyon Labor Camp, in the summer of 1949)

SOLDAN

I thought it was just idle talk when the men claimed that Soldan once gulped down a whole bucket of cabbage soup in front of the duty officer.

He was a tall, thin man, with sleepy watery-gray eyes. As a free man, he had been assistant engineer on passenger trains running between Tartu and Valga. He claimed that he had always eaten three loaves of brown bread on each trip. In spite of that, he had been just as thin as a free man.

While assigned to his brigade, I had to translate his protests about the insufficiency of his rations to the bread weigher every morning. Whenever he gauged his 200-gram portion of bread between his fingers, he would always suspect he was being cheated. All his protests fell on deaf ears, because I neglected to translate a single one of his Estonian curse words. Whenever he became intolerably insistent, I would break off a piece of my own rations, which he immediately stuffed in his mouth. Only then would he be quiet.

The bread distributor noticed what I was doing. He began watching me.

One morning, when I try to pass the bread window without taking out my rations, the bread weigher stops me, asking: "Why aren't you taking out your rations?"

It is my second day of penalty rations. The brigade commander has assigned me only 25% of my usual quantity for the work I have done, and for this ten-day period, I was to receive only 500 grams of bread daily. On the first day, I took my bread rations before leaving for work, and nibbled at it from my jacket pocket during the workday until it was all gone. By the evening, I was hungry. And since I did not want to go to bed hungry again, I decided not to take out my rations until the evening, when we were brought back to the camp. I explain my sad situation to that young Ukrainian by the bread window. He gazes at me sympathetically and says: "Have some crumbs." I ask him: "Are you sure I can have some?"

"Well, let's see," he replies meaningfully. He weighs out tiny morsels of bread that have been trimmed from the others' rations. The pile already weighs five hundred grams, but the good man keeps piling crumbs onto the scale. "That's enough!" I chide him quietly. "You'll get in trouble!" But he replies: "Be quiet!" When he feels he has given me enough, he tells me to stuff it into my hat. In this act, I can see nothing but God's wondrous concern for me, His assurance that I would not suffer innocently for the humiliation that the brigade commander has heaped upon me. My tobacco ration must be used to save my countryman's life.

The Lord is setting my table in the presence of mine enemies. An ancient poet sang the same song of his own experience.

I continue sharing my meager portion with Soldan every day. But it does little to bring us closer. His insatiety annoys me, and I sometimes criticize him sharply for it. His inability to repay me troubles him. Time and again, he manages to find a handful of breadcrumbs and half a herring to give me, and that makes him feel better. And so we live in kind of an odd friendship. I do not want to say that this friendship lasted until the day that the brigade commander assigned Soldan to be my unit's leader.

One day, we are to start erecting scaffolding around the factory. The factory is to undergo refurbishing. We haul planks and boards from the sawmill up to the top of the hill. Soldan is a dutiful worker. He is particularly diligent, because now, as group leader, he is being trusted. Occasionally, I invite him to sit and rest for a while. But his sense of duty forbids him to do so. I sit on a rock as he remains standing, without letting go of his end of the board. It takes us half a day to finally carry up all the scaffolding materials. Now we start erecting the framework around the factory walls. Neither of us have ever put up scaffolding, but we have to do it now. We are terribly tired from hauling the lumber, and we talk to each other very little, but we are making good progress. We set some planks upright, connect them with transverse boards, and soon complete the bottom section of one side of the framework. As we are lifting the first board onto the framework, the foreman suddenly appears. He is a tall man, a free worker of a few words, a man who has already served his time as a criminal prisoner. As soon as Soldan catches sight of the foreman, he does something so odd that it leaves me speechless. The assertiveness of a superior suddenly wells up inside him. All day, he has not been able to assert his position as team leader. Whenever he tries to boss me around, I simply ignore him. I take a handful of breadcrumbs from my pocket and eat. I give Soldan a handful as well, and all peace is restored. But now we are in the presence of a stranger who outranks us. The man is not particularly interested in what we are doing. However, a string of colorful obscenities that are now being blurted out in badly broken Russian attracts his attention. The foreman is forced to inquire what is the matter. In praise of Soldan, I have to say that he has learned very little Russian in the camp, with the exception of curse words. The poor man is now forced to swear and shout at me in Estonian, because this is how a superior talks to his underling, and Soldan must now assert himself in the presence of the foreman, using all manner of obscenities directed at me. It is his way of assuring his superior that everything is going well.

Soldan's behavior has me so completely stunned that I forget my good manners and plop down onto a boulder in view of both my superiors. Since I do not say a word, and since the foreman has no idea what is going on, I have to be the intermediary. Soldan continues foaming at the mouth, and so the foreman turns to me, asking: "Do either of you numbskulls understand Russian?"

I reply to the foreman: "Excuse me, but neither one of us is a numbskull. Look at the kind of work we're doing. We have carried all these materials here ourselves. Now we're putting up the scaffolding. We are terribly tired. But still, we'd like to finish our job by nightfall. The unit leader is a compatriot of mine, and he lost his nerve when he saw you approaching. He was afraid you'll start cursing at us. We've noticed that all the supervisors curse. And here, there is nobody else but me to curse at, so he's saving you the trouble."

The tall galoot of a foreman sits on a beam, listening. He listens to me carefully, but says nothing. He finally gets up, takes a pack of "Belomor" cigarettes from his pocket, hands me a cigarette, steps over to Soldan, pats him on the shoulder and says: "You're a real dick of a supervisor." And nothing more. He is already gone.

"Did you hear what he said to you, brother?" I ask Soldan, after the foreman has gone. "You must know enough Russian to understand what he said."

Yes, he knows enough Russian. And it makes him think. Two weeks later, as we are loading lumber at the bread house on one of my days off, Soldan asks me: "What did you tell that foreman that time we were building the scaffolding?" I prefer not to bring that up again, and I answer: "You'd do better to ask me what I didn't say to him." Soldan puzzled over that response for more than two weeks.

I had started going to the bread house with Soldan to make up some work on my day off. My good friend, the secretary of the Baptist League, Grigori Ilyich Kashirski was baking bread. He received us heartily. On that day, we could eat as much bread as we wanted. After we had cut boards for a while, Grigori Ilyich brought us two loaves of bread as encouragement. Soldan wolfed down his portion immediately. I nibbled a bit of mine. Around lunchtime, Kashirski brought each of us another half a loaf. Without further ado, Soldan gobbled that down as well, in addition to the part of my loaf left over from that morning.

After we finished working, each of us got another loaf of bread, fresh from the oven. Even before we had assembled at the camp gates with the rest of the men who had worked on their day off, Soldan had finished off every last crumb. I could not figure out where he put all this food, and finally gave up trying. His belly showed not the slightest slight bulge beneath his quilted jacket.

Another time, he surprised me even more. On a day off, I was shingling the kitchen hut's roof. The cook rewards me with a bowl of porridge and a mug of tea. The Azerbaijani cook is very pleased with my dedication and asks if I have a countryman who might know how to whitewash his room. He would be well fed for it. I immediately think of Soldan. And Soldan is more than willing to give up his day of rest, even though he has never done any whitewashing. But why not – it would be a grave injustice to his belly if he let this opportunity slip by. And so we establish a good relationship with the cooks. There is more than enough food to fill my belly. The cook even gives me a crock of tea which I take up to the roof for an occasional gulp to soothe my throat. Soldan is so busy all day that he does not come outside for fresh air even once.

The summer days in Kolyma are quite long. The sun absolutely refuses to set behind the mountains. The evening shift is already entering the gates. But it feels so good to work quietly and alone on this roof that I do not want to climb down. Climbing down is quite a feat, because we have no decent ladders. One time, that created something of a problem. Up on the roof, I felt the urge to urinate. Well, no problem, I did my business up there. And suddenly, horrible cursing erupted from beneath the rafters. Cursing a blue streak, someone was shouting about water dripping from the rafters although there is no rain falling from a cloudless sky. The overseer had been slouched on a bench under the rafters digesting his second helping. Fearing the worst, I clambered behind the roof ridge to hide, and the overseer was left to puzzle over the origins of the mysterious rain shower.

After the evening shift has been fed, and the men are returning to their huts, a tired voice calls from below: "Harri, come down!"

I had been planning to do so anyway. Once I climb down, I am met by a rather forlorn-looking Soldan. He approaches me with an unusual offer: "Would you like some porridge? I have some left over!"

"Well, well, that's unheard of! You have some left over?" I cannot hide my amazement.

"But this is my ninth bowlful," says Soldan, groaning.

And then I noticed that those eight bowls of millet porridge had distended his belly quite noticeably. This would be a lot harder to manage than a bucket of cabbage soup at the O.P. He was not going to get rid of this meal quite as fast.

But I could not eat the porridge, because I had stuffed myself with an extra helping of my own.

He finally relinquished his portion to the boilerman Kalbus, an old man from Võru County. Kalbus's eyes opened wide as he declared: "Well, well, Soldan, you're actually full. That's something I've never heard before."

(Canyon Labor Camp, in the summer of 1949)

JUST DON'T COMPLAIN!

"Just don't complain!" admonished Grigori Ilyich, after I had poured my heart out to him yet again.

And I truly did not want to complain. But when you are constantly surrounded by reminders of the injustice you have suffered, you tend to complain in spite of yourself.

I gradually realized that unless God Himself came to help me, my complaints might drive me to the abyss of despair once again.

But that Ossetian brigade commander is keeping me on penalty rations for another ten-day period. He is still trying to extort my packet of *makhorka* that I had promised to Kala. But he will not get it, even if he puts me on the slackers' list for yet a third ten-day period.

My bread-weighing friend has the day off, and I get only 500 grams at the bread window. By the time I return that night, there is not a crumb left. The workday has been hard, and the bowlful of soup I gulp down without bread does more to stimulate my hunger than to satisfy it.

"God, are you really letting me go to bed hungry tonight?" That is the preface to my prayer as I climb up onto my bunk. I have already forgotten the wise admonition: "Just don't complain!". I should not complain, even when I suffer from hunger.

As I lie down, worms of sullenness begin to gnaw at my heart. With a heart like this, I can find no way to send a prayer of gratitude to the Lord for having survived a day like this one. And yet, I am to experience something quite unusual. Suddenly, I feel someone pulling on my big toe.

"Harri, are you asleep yet?" says a young Estonian boy from the floor. He has come from Barrack 4 to look for me. He is the only Estonian working in the maintenance brigade, which repairs apartments in the free workers' settlement. They need a stencil right away, and they have no one who can draw one. The Estonian boy recalled his compatriot from Barrack 7. I had occasionally made some carvings and drawn pictures for the men. Could I come to their barrack and draw them a stencil, which they could use to adorn the walls of rooms for free workers' settlement residents?

I do not let him cajole me for long. I quickly climb down from my bunk, put on my boots and go to Barrack 4. The men are not even thinking of going to sleep yet. It is eminently obvious that they are not enduring the brutal slavery that is breaking us, the men of the construction brigade. We are pushed relentlessly for all the 14 hours of our workday. The Ukrainian brigade commander explains what kind of stencil they need to finish their work. I draw it for them. I make two stencils, with flowers and leaves, and cut them out as well.

I toil on the stencils for an hour and a half. The men stare curiously at my artwork. The brigade commander assesses my work with a knowing eye and voices his approval with a single word: "*Dobre*"[34] ("Good"). I am glad I can enhance my compatriot's reputation for helping his brigade commander through a difficult time. As I leave, I say to these strangers: "Good night."

But the brigade commander will not let me leave just yet: "Wait, I want to pay you for your work."

I: "What can you give me?"

Brigade commander: "I can give you a ration of bread."

I: "Thanks, but I won't eat the bread ration that belongs to you."

Brigade commander: "We get so much bread from the free workers' settlement that all our men have more than enough rations."

I: "Well, that's different. In that case, I thank you kindly. I am rather hungry."

When the strangers see me accepting the bread with such joyous excitement, they must think I have a hearty appetite. One of them goes to the head of his bed, pulls out a bread ration and says: "Take this one too."

---

34 *dobre* – Ukrainian for "good"

"Thank you very much, but my services are not worth that much," I say, trying to be polite.

But my modesty drives another man to hand me his bread ration as well. I cannot even hold all the loaves anymore, and the crumbs that they have re-attached to the loaves with wood splinters are crumbling off. I pull off my *gymnastiorka*[35] tunic and carefully wrap my "salary" in it. By the door, yet another bread ration is added to my bundle. And so I step happily into the white summer night[36], as happy as any person who has just witnessed the glorious miracle of God's grace could ever be. I walk across the camp yard, feeling as if I should lift my voice in a loud song of praise. I thank Him, happy as a child receiving Christmas presents; all I can do is to tell God what I am feeling in my heart. Not until my barrack threshold do I remember that I have not yet asked God's forgiveness for the complaining with which I disappointed Him just a short while ago.

Not all the men are asleep yet. I wave to them as I enter the barrack with my bundle. They approach me curiously. And they each receive a piece of bread in return for a hearty thank-you.

And I do not have to fall asleep hungry. Oh, how often we people will start complaining before we need to, and without good reason!

But I have learned a valuable lesson.

I used to think that I could describe God's grace only by preaching powerful sermons from the pulpit. Now, I have learned to truly experience God's grace. He came and blessed me with a bit of bread when I was hungry, with a warm handshake when I felt myself forsaken, and with a quiet moment within the din of the barrack, when I could reach Him more solemnly with a solitary prayer than with a whole pulpitful of sermons.

Thank you for everything! I tried to impress the tremendous value of the maxim "Just don't complain!" deep into my heart.

(Canyon Labor Camp, in the summer of 1949)

---

35 *gymnastiorka* – Soldier's blouse-type shirt; typical of long, belted slipover peasant tops

36 *white night* – Special light of long summer evenings in Arctic regions

REVENGE

I saw it all from the kitchen roof, where I was spending my day off. I was shingling the roof at the request of the cooks in exchange for a bowlful of porridge.

A truck stops at the gates of the camp. A man wearing a terribly dusty *fufaika* gets out. Apparently, he has come a long way. He disappears into the guardhouse for some time. The guards, armed with automatic weapons, climb back into the truck, which drives off, throwing up clouds of dust.

I hear excited voices down in the kitchen. Someone is shouting loudly in broken Russian. That must be the Azerbaijani cook. He has a booming voice like that. But I wonder who he is yelling at. The mess hall commander Muradeyev, a Tartar, rushes across the camp yard toward the kitchen. He and the Azerbaijani cook are fast friends. He has sensed that something is wrong in the kitchen again. A month ago, a Russian had stabbed one of the cooks, who was also dark-skinned and hailed from somewhere by the Caspian Sea. Now, all the rest of the cooks are very vigilant. They no longer let any strangers cross the kitchen threshold. Someone might attack them again in the name of a second helping. It does not matter to me, I have a good relationship with the cooks since I started working for them, and Zunayev can taunt me with his penalty rations until the eve of my death.

And so I ignore the agitated voices emanating from the kitchen and continue hammering my shingles. The unfinished roof is covered with tarpaulin. I gently roll the tarpaulin forward, making good progress with the new roof. Suddenly, two men run out of the kitchen. One is holding a knife, the other, an axe. At first, I can not make out who they are and where they are going. Then, I recognize the Azerbaijani cook and the mess hall commander. Turning around, I see a man leave the guardhouse and stroll calmly down the camp roll call line toward the barracks. It is that same dusty man who was dropped off by the truck at the camp gates. Now he has taken off his quilted jacket and is shaking the dust from it as he walks.

Suddenly, the man stops and changes direction. He is no longer approaching the mess tent, but is headed for the first aid station. Perhaps he is going to get some medicine from the medical attendant to relieve the stress and strain of his long trip. He has barely taken ten steps when the two men attack him. It happens so suddenly that I can not figure out how they got all the way over there. And then, it all happens quickly. The Tartar smashes the blunt end of the axe directly onto the newcomer's head. The man screams once and collapses in the yard. Then, the Azerbaijani cook gets to work with his long kitchen knife. I cannot watch any more. Later, I hear that they found 17 knife wounds in the man's body. That dark-skinned Asiatic had really tried to make goulash out of that poor man, in the truest sense of the word. After butchering that dusty man, they calmly walk over to the guardhouse to report their courageous act. And then, the guards, who I suspect have watched the entire scene unfold from the guardhouse window, finally come out to the scene.

After I climb down from the roof, I ask another dark-skinned cook about the meaning of all this. His explanation is simple: "Revenge. You know, my countryman, it is customary for the Caucasian peoples. Whenever someone harms us, we must take revenge on him. This *suka* killed one of our comrades, and now we killed him. Don't feel sorry for him. He deserved it."

All right then, if he deserves it, I will try not to feel sorry for him. But the more I think about this incident, the better I understand it. After his trial, the unfortunate man was sent back to the same camp in which he committed his crime, so that he could be slaughtered.

Both avengers were placed in isolation cells and soon thereafter removed from our camp. That autumn, when I was sent from the Canyon to Laxos, I found them both already there. The Azerbaijani was working as the chief cook, and the Tartar as the mess hall manager. And they found work for me in the kitchen once again. But here, I did not need those second helpings quite so much, because now I started receiving packages from my homeland.

HE IS A BLACKCOAT[37]

The young Ukrainian rebel had been assigned to lead the group of men putting up electrical posts. Zugaev ordered him to select six men from the brigade himself. The boy was friendly toward me, and he asked if I wanted to go "walking" in the free workers' settlement. I had no objections, although my illness had left me feeling rather weak. The boy reassured me that the job was not very hard, and besides – sometimes they got lucky. The people in the free workers' settlement were said to be generous in sharing their bread with the prisoners, and they even gave some of them *makhorka*. People in the free workers' settlement also received packages. I never received anything, and the brigade commander continued to taunt me, one ten-day period after another, with the penalty rations. All right, I would join the "lucky" group. But I found the first day daunting. An armed guard always followed us closely. We could not go begging at a single door, and I was so busy that I barely had time to wipe my nose. The work was murderous. My pickaxe quickly got dull, useless for digging any deeper than half a meter. I had to chop a trench from which I could continue digging. We had no crowbars, although they would hardly have made our work any easier. By nighttime, all my muscles and bones ached as if they had been crushed by a steamroller. When I complained to my group leader that he had tricked me by inviting me to engage in this murderous slave labor, he assured me that "You won't have to dig holes every day."

---

37 *blackcoat* – Clergyman; a derogatory reference to traditional clerical garb

The next day, we were to bring in the posts and stand them upright. But there is nowhere to bring them from. There are no mature timber forests growing in the canyon. The posts have to be brought in from someplace farther south. Supposedly, they had been hauled in by tractor sled in wintertime. I could not imagine how they would now be hauled to the settlement. And transportation issues are not my problem. My superiors would certainly know what had to be done. We have no lumber, which means that all we can do is sit around. We sit by a barrack that looks like some kind of dormitory. Cans and scraps of food have been tossed out of the barrack, and now lie a few feet away from us. A couple of the men in our group ask the guard for permission to go urinate over there. He says all right, because the area is visible from his post. Just in case, he puts his automatic weapon on his lap. But the men, instead of responding to nature's call, quickly grab something from the trash pile and come back. The tall Lithuanian forest ranger triumphantly shows me two heels of bread that he has stuffed into his coat. Apparently, this is a well-supplied trash bin. I also ask the guard for permission to answer nature's call. He lets me. Over there, I see another discarded piece of bread, but do not pick it up. Someone has also thrown out a handful of tiny radishes. I gather them up and stick them in my pocket. Later, I wash them in the stream by our camp and eat them. They are the only fresh vegetables I eat until my release from the camps. For seven years, I did not taste a single potato, with the exception of a double handful of dried potato slices that a free worker in Lazo brought me in exchange for a coffin I had made for his dead child.

But they never let our forces sit idle for long. Suddenly, a foreman appears out of nowhere. He swears at the group leader for not hauling away the support posts that have been lying by the sawmill for days. He claims they should have been carried over to the settlement yesterday. However, none of us had even seen the foreman yesterday. Since the group leader does not protest this unjust scolding with a single word, I assume he may actually have received such an order from the foreman. Once his superior leaves, our group leader mutters: "F--- him. I've never seen him before, and this is the first time I've heard of these posts. Well, all right, let's carry them up here!" The guard orders us to get up and walk to the sawmill two-by-two in front of him. On the bridge, two sentries count us twice before we are allowed to enter the work zone. The same drill is repeated on our return. The posts earmarked for the electrification of the free workers' houses are stacked by the sawmill. There are about 30, each one four meters long and 70 millimeters thick. There is little discussion about what we should do. Each one of us has to heave a post onto our shoulder and line up. The strapping young Lithuanian schoolboy heaves two posts onto his shoulder. This inspires the guard, who exhorts us: "Are you really weaker than he is? Each of you carry two!" The men take this as an order. Some of them pick up another post out of fear, others, out of vanity. I must follow suit. The one post is pressing painfully into my shoulder; how can I possibly carry two? With great effort, I carry both over the bridge, where we take our first break. However, I know I cannot carry both posts all the way back at once. I ask the guard if I may go on ahead with one timber and return later for the other, because carrying both together is too much for me. After some hesitation, the *komsomolets* agrees. He says: "All right, get going!" The others stay there, and I set off with my one post. I carry this timber for about 100 meters, and then I return for the other one. In the interval, the guard has changed his mind. He says: "You, blackcoat, are just fooling around, pretending you don't have the strength. You've lived the good life, doing nothing but swinging your censer around. Now you must learn how to work. No special exceptions for you. We will go on, and you will carry both posts. You'll manage just fine."

Stunned, I stare at the guard, and look around my group in great amazement. How does this red-epauletted man know I am a cleric? Which one of the men has told him? I do not want to think badly of any one of them. When we reach the spot where I left my first post, the guard orders me to heave it onto my shoulder. All the men wait, their faces serious. Only Paplavicius snickers: "So what's the problem? It's like carrying little twigs."

With great effort, I heave the other "twig" onto my shoulder and follow the other men. It is grueling work. I clench my teeth and keep walking. But my exhausted body cannot withstand the exertion. Suddenly, everything goes black, and I collapse into a heap, timbers and all. The men rush over and help me back to my feet. Even Paplavicius stops snickering. The incident seems to have surprised even the guard. Finally, he asks: "Do you have the strength to continue?"

"I'll try," I respond.

He lets me continue with only one post at a time, even though I did not ask him if I could. I return for the other one when the others sit down to take a break.

That night, the tall Lithuanian forest ranger tells me: "My countryman Paplavicius is a pig. He doesn't know what life is all about. He was already behind bars as a schoolboy. And now he doesn't know how to behave. Please don't hate our people because of him."

No, I do not hate their people, or Paplavicius either.

The next day, I am able to prove it.

It is a good day for us. The posts have still not arrived. But they are to arrive "soon, very soon." We sit in the middle of the free workers' settlement, in the yard of a house where we have dug one of the holes into which we will place the first post. Although it is a summer day, a peculiar coolness flows at us from somewhere in the mountains. The family living in the house has gone off to work, so we cannot hope that anyone might offer us something to eat. The residents have hauled a pile of tree stumps into the yard. Chopping these stumps into firewood will take a lot of hard work. We have a saw and axe. To pass the time, I start sawing and chopping up the stumps. For a while, the men watch me silently. Finally, the group leader says: "Good *batya*, nobody is going to pay you for that."

But I am not working on the stumps in the hopes that someone might pay me for it. By way of explanation, I reply: "I'm doing this for the satisfaction of knowing I've done a good deed for someone."

The group leader falls silent; most of the men have no idea what I am talking about. Only the guard, who is with us for the first time, stares at me in disbelief. Paplavicius has not had a chance to tell him who I am yet.

We wait for the posts for a long time. I keep on sawing and chopping. The stack is growing little by little as I keep adding firewood.

Finally, the foreman appears and takes us away. The posts have been hauled into place. We start carrying them to the holes. The posts have been dumped by the side of the road, about 500 meters from the first hole. We decide to carry them into place and put them up one by one. Before picking up our first post, we take a smoke break. Someone has some cheap tobacco in the pocket of his quilted coat, with which he rolls a single cigarette for the entire group. Once we finish smoking, the work takes us quite a while. It takes seven men to carry the first post. We rest three times before we get it to the hole. While the men are taking their smoke break, I continue chopping up the stumps. The others watch idly as one man shovels dirt to fill the post hole. I am still sawing and chopping.

The lady of the house appears from somewhere. She looks at the standing post and says something stiffly to the guard. She is unlocking the padlock on her door when her gaze suddenly stops at the stack of firewood. With a kind expression, she turns to all of us and nods. "She told you 'thanks'!" snickers Paplavicius. "You too," mumbles the tall forest ranger. No more is said.

We have set the post upright and the hole has been filled. One of the men asks: "I wonder if that is enough for today?" The group leader thinks it is not enough. We should erect another post. Before we go over to fetch it, we take a smoke break without the smoke, because nobody has any tobacco. And then the lady of the house appears. She is carrying a bowl. She asks the guard if she may give us something. The quiet man nods. The lady lays down a cloth, onto which she places a bowl of blueberries with sugar, a bit of bread, and some cheap tobacco wadded up in paper.

The first to lunge for the goodies is Paplavicius. But the forest ranger grabs him by the scruff and barks: "Where do you think you're going? We can have some of this only if *batya* says so. He did all the work himself." But the other men are not nearly as restrained. Soon, they surround the loot, and the group leader says: "*Batya*, you may have one extra handful of berries, because you didn't smoke."

I can have a little something extra! I could actually drive them all away from the bowl. But I have told them that I was not doing the work in expectation of getting paid. I must be good to my word, and so I say: "Take whatever you want, and leave behind whatever you think my portion should be."

And they left something in the bowl for me.

(Canyon Labor Camp, in the summer of 1949.)

THE WOODCARVING PASTOR

Korol had been taken away to some recovery camp. But his name was so renowned that it was often on everyone's lips. He had been a supreme artisan. One had to give a thumbs-up whenever they spoke his title. This meant – a master *par excellence*. The Lithuanians themselves did not consider him to be a special star, because nearly every older Lithuanian could carve crosses out of toothbrush sticks. They showed the works of this Lithuanian carver to me. Most of them were aluminum cigarette cases, with rather unimpressive engravings that were adorned with bits of colored plastic melted into the design. Judging from his work, he was a proficient master, but a rather poor artist. After I had seen his work, I summoned the courage to try my hand at wood carving in the Canyon. At the Magadan Transit Camp it had made me so famous that I held my head high whenever I was asked for my specialty. I am a pastor and a woodcarver. And this despite the fact that neither skill was of particular use in the camps.

When the PPT chief came by to assign the fresh group of prisoners their jobs upon their arrival at the Canyon, he wanted to know everyone's specialty. When I told him I was a woodcarving pastor, he became so confused that he admitted publicly that he had never heard of a profession like that before. But it helped him remember me. He scratched his head for some time, trying to figure out where he could place a man with such an unusual profession. Finally, he found the appropriate position for me in the construction shop, which needed two cabinetmakers. Several cabinetmakers had been brought into the Canyon with our transport, but he considered me to be more important than just any cabinetmaker, since he assumed I was skilled the fine art of woodworking. The other man assigned to work in the carpentry shop was the Lithuanian architect Vasilauskas. The two of us were to become the most highly qualified master cabinetmakers in this camp. The real cabinetmakers were sent below the earth to mine cobalt.

On the night of our arrival, after roll call, we are taken to the barrack to meet our brigade and its commander, i.e. those who will take us to the mess hall bread line the next morning and then to the gates by the guardhouse for assignment into groups.

When we arrive at the work zone on the hill, the workshop manager shows us to a workbench where we are to plane parts of a window frame. But he soon finds out that neither of us has ever held a plane in our hands. All his foul oaths do little to remedy the situation. This must be some terrible, regrettable mistake. Neither of us claimed to be cabinetmakers. Until things can be straightened out, we are sent to the sawmill as substitute workers. The group leader for the sawmill crew is an Estonian named Malik. He is a fresh-faced, kindhearted boy from Haapsalu, who can find us nothing else to do but to roll logs from the stack down to the saw frame.

We are both tall, thin men who have done little physical labor in our lifetime. They need strong men in a place like this. Together, we try to lift the logs from the stack onto the crossbeams, which would allow the logs to roll downward, but we lack the strength. The log does not even budge. What now? I go tell our troubles to Malik. He comes over and, seeing how hard we are trying, bursts out laughing. He brings a crowbar and lever. He uses the crowbar to shift the log just a bit, and then tells us to place the lever under it. What a difference! Now either of us can toss the massive logs from the stack and set them rolling. Our thanks to the man who taught us this trick so quickly.

With great enthusiasm, we set about doing our new job. Soon, however, our bodies are drenched with sweat, and we realize that the job is not quite as easy as it had seemed. After we roll a sufficient number of logs down to the saw frame, we cannot even think of sitting down. The sawdust bin is rather small and must be emptied constantly. That is also our job. And the wood slivers must be carried to a stack about one hundred meters away. By the time we finally finish that job, they are placing the last of our logs onto the saw frame. The sawing progresses with frightening speed. As we start rolling new logs down, we are already weak-kneed. My palms are so torn up with splinters that they are wracked with a searing pain whenever I pick up the crowbar. And now we have an accident. I do not know how that tall Lithuanian managed to leave his foot under a log. Suddenly, he yells and lets go of the lever. Fortunately, I am holding the crowbar. Bearing down with all my strength, I manage to free his foot from beneath the log. He is no longer of any use as a worker. Nobody has time to fetch the medical attendant from the work zone. And what good would that do, anyway? I pull off his laced boot and see that his toes, although not broken, begin to swell visibly and turn dark blue. The pressure has obviously been too hard for such a delicate man. I fashion a compress out of a rag which I dip in cold water and wrap around his toes. Then I leave my partner sitting on the end of a beam and start rolling the logs down to the saw frame by myself.

It takes tremendous effort to get each log from the stack and send it, by repeatedly running back and forth down the length of the log, down the proper pathway. Soon, I am so exhausted that I envy Vasilauskas for his swollen toes. But I will not injure myself deliberately. Tears welling up in my eyes, I sigh to God, whom I had once described in a sermon as a source of strength to the weary, and pick up the crowbar once again. It seems to me that lunchtime, a chance for a brief rest, should have come long ago. But lunchtime simply would not come.

Finally, the saw frame is turned off. Now I feel I have earned the right to rest my back. I sit next to my partner on the beam. His pain seems to have subsided, but he cannot even think of pulling his boot on.

Malik calls us to come and eat the porridge that has been brought for our brigade. I do not want to get up for anything, but I must do so for the sake of my injured partner. When Malik is met with silence at his question about how I am feeling, he whispers: "You won't be doing much more work today. The saw frame is usually still after lunch." Astonished, I stare at him and ask naively: "How is that possible?" Confidently, Malik responds: "Everything is possible in the camps."

He is a fine boy, that Malik. He knows how to break the saw frame as well as he knows how to fix it. That day, the saw frame really does refuse to start up again. Oddly enough, nobody comes by to swear about it. That evening, we stumble home together with the others in our shift, like the two highly qualified specialists that we are. One of us holds his boot in his hand and limps hard as he holds my arm.

The next morning, they do not take me back to the lumbermen's' crew. My brigade commander hands me his wooden cigarette case and asks: "Can you make something on here?"

I assess the lid and find it to be too thin. Nothing can be carved into it.

"That's no problem," says the brigade commander. "Tell me how thick the lid should be," he asks me, the expert. I say: "It should be five millimeters."

"All right, it will have a new lid by this evening," the brigade commander assures me. On this new lid, I carve mountains and a bear and the moon. I paint and polish them too. The brigade commander shows it off to everyone and boasts: "Look! Our camp has a new Korol."

One day I am summoned to see the foreman. The camp commander has heard about the new Korol at his camp. Would I like to make his wife a carved sewing box? I say I would be glad to, but I do not know how to make hinges. It would be best if a cabinetmaker made the box, and I would adorn it with carvings. The deal is made. And one day, all the hinged box sections are brought to me. It is lovely beechwood, waiting for a master's hand. I tell the foreman that this is time-consuming work and that I will not have time to make it at the barrack after regular work hours, since no one is allowed to have any sharp instruments there. With the consent of the regime commander, I am allowed to set up my workshop in the foreman's quarters. The machine shop has made me some chisels, but my main tool is still my shoemaker's knife. But since my work progresses slowly due to lack of time, the foreman decides to let me stay in the camp zone for a few days. The doctor writes out a medical excuse for me, and I sit in the foreman's room and carve a sewing box for the camp commander's wife. On the sides, I have drawn wolves chasing deer; on the lid, a child feeding a roedeer. These figures have a symbolic meaning, which I never reveal to anyone. Who knows what new torments they would devise for me; I was already serving time for some mysterious "crimes" I was not aware I had committed.

It felt good to sit in that warm room and conjure figures into wood. If I had proper woodcarving instruments, my work would not have been nearly as time-consuming or as hard on my patience.

The foreman's attendant is a student from the Department of Philology from Vilnius. He comes by and talks to me occasionally. This Lithuanian, who claims that his mother is Latvian, is a rather smart young man. He also understands a bit of Estonian. Soon, we become good friends. But then, he tries to do me a favor that proves to be fateful. From the kitchen, he brings me a bowlful of porridge swimming in mutton fat. I eat it heartily. I have not tasted anything this delicious in a long time. But a few hours later, I regret my gluttony. My stomach is wracked with pain, and soon my digestive system is as upset as it can be. At this time, a wave of dysentery is sweeping our camp. I go to the clinic. The inpatient clinic is already crowded with so many men that there is no bed space for me. My compatriot, the doctor, gives me the best medications available, including a little box of rose hips, but none of this helps my digestive system. I begin to fast. For the first few days, it feels terrible to starve myself. But I pray for strength from God, who tells us that bad blood will leave a person only with prayer and fasting, and who has himself set an example for us with His 40-day fast in the solitude of the desert. I give Soldan my bread rations, soup and porridge. In exchange, he gives me his tea. And two 200-gram servings of tea are all that I allow myself to ingest over nine days. On the tenth and eleventh day, I eat a bit of toasted bread. And when I feel that it will no longer cause any problems, I gradually return to my regular diet.

I am now very thin. On one of my free days, I help haul reindeer meat to a warehouse outside the prison camp. I am so weak that I can barely stand up. The warehouse keeper decides to weigh me, just for fun. We calculate that my naked weight must be about 49, but no more than 50 kilograms. But I go to work every day, because I have no fever. Even as the fever sets in, I continue my carving work. My job is finally completed, and I hand the nicely polished item over to the camp commander. The foreman is as proud as if he had made the box himself. The camp commander asks about the significance of the carved, embossed figures. I simply say: "They are drawn on the box very clearly; everyone can see what they are." The camp commander does not want to look stupid, and silently takes the box under his arm. He neglects to say "thank you," because the work has been done by a slave who deserves no such unnecessary courtesy. The foreman will undoubtedly be given a handful of *makhorka* for my efforts.

I no longer have to inflate my importance by emphasizing my artistry at woodcarving, because one day, Korol returns. He is a simple, kindhearted Lithuanian farm boy, who had learned the art of carving from his father. When he sees my drawings, he asks me to draw him something too.

From that time onward, he begins honing his skills according to the patterns I draw for him. In this way, we form a two-man workshop. I draw the designs, and he carves them into wood or aluminum. But we are given little time to admire each other's artistry, and the joy of our superiors in our cooperative venture is short-lived. Soon, I am hustled to a transport and taken to the camp where I should have ended up in the first place, according to my official papers. However, our transport had been rerouted to the Canyon, which lay in the middle of the free workers' settlement at Factory #3, very close to Lazo. Now, after half a year's stay at the Canyon, I reach my proper destination. Once again, my strange specialty and I stand before the PPT chief. It saves me from the subterranean work. I become the construction workshop's toolkeeper.

(Canyon Labor Camp, September 1949)

YOU ARE MY CHRISTIAN BROTHER!

I still have my New Testament. It is a priceless treasure. Time and again, someone asks me to read from it.

One morning, after returning from the mess tent, several of my countrymen and I lie on the top bunk. The crowding has gradually given way to more breathing room in the barrack. Every week, men were being taken away on transports. Now we, the members of an undemanding nation, finally have a warmer spot to lie on.

Once again, I am holding my beloved book, from which I am reading passages and explaining them to the men. Suddenly, a tall Uzbek with slanted eyes and prominent cheekbones is standing before us. He asks me with a strong eastern accent: "Countryman, what are you reading there?"

"The Christian Koran," I reply.

"What does it say?"

"It talks about the same God as the Islamic Koran."

"Do you believe in Allah?"

"Allah, il-Allah!" I reply with pathos, holding up two fingers in the Islamic salute.

"But does your Koran say anything about Allah?"

"Of course it does."

"Read it to me!" orders the Muslim.

And I interpret the 23rd psalm of David for him like this: "Allah is my shepherd, I shall not want. Allah makes me lie down in green pastures; he leads me beside still waters."

He listens with visible excitement, but stops me abruptly: "Hold it!" And he disappears without a word.

"Did you say something he didn't like?" wonder the men. Lacking fluency in Russian, they understood very little of our conversation.

A few minutes later, my fellow sufferer, the Uzbek, returns. He has brought along another broad-faced Muslim, and explains to him in broken Russian that he has found a Christian mullah with a Koran that talks about Allah.

Now my congregation includes two Muslims. One of them is a mullah. The mullah desperately wants his compatriot to hear stories from the Christian Koran. Since the other man understands Russian very poorly, the mullah has to translate much of it into Uzbek. And so I spend time every day introducing the secrets of the Christian Koran to the two Muslims. They actually listen with greater eagerness than my own Estonian brethren. And yet, they ask me nothing. If something is unclear, they discuss the issue in their own language, which I do not understand at all.

Now, after translating the New Testament and the Psalms for these Muslims for nearly two weeks, I suddenly realize I should attempt some missionary work with these two. Perhaps I might succeed in converting them to the beatific Christian faith. However, the history of missionary work shows that Muslims are the most difficult to evangelize, and that missionaries have been the least successful in Muslim-populated areas.

I contemplate my approach, not wanting to frighten them with my intentions nor to let them slam shut the door to their hearts.

I realize it would be most appropriate to praise their existing convictions. I begin one of our meetings by saying: "From what I know of Islamic morality, it is more rigorously upheld in Islam than in any other religion." They are pleased by the acknowledgement. As if returning the kindness, one of them asks me to tell them something about Christian morality. What better way to do so than to read them the Sermon on the Mount. They listen attentively without asking for any explanation. When I reach the part where Jesus tells us to love our enemies, my Muslim friends launch into a loud discussion in Uzbek. Apparently, they find something about this to be quite unacceptable. I ask them what the problem is, and the mullah replies: "This is not what the Koran teaches us." Apparently, they have been listening to my book as if it were a chapter of the Koran. All I had read to them was perfectly suited to the world view of followers of the Koran, except for the command to love your enemies.

I ask them: "How does the Koran handle this command?"

The mullah says: "We know that our hearts must be open to our brothers, and we must set our table for strangers, and we must offer them protection under our roof, but for our enemies, we have nothing but our swords at the ready."

"All right, but doesn't the Koran say: If you want to kill your enemy, you need only to strike a blow with your sword; if you want to vanquish your enemy, you must give him your heart."

That argument confuses them once more, and again they engage in loud debate. When they are silent once again, I ask why this excited them so.

"These things are contradictory," explains the mullah.

And then I must explain to them the wisdom of Islam in the light of the Gospels. I ask them which victory would be sweeter for them – one in which the victors come to a defeated land, full of nothing but ruins and stinking corpses, or a land in which the victor can walk with yesterday's enemy as if with a brother.

Naturally, they admit that the latter victory is the better one.

"Well, you see, the prerequisite for such a victory is to obey the order to love your enemy. It would not be possible any other way," I explain.

I can see the Muslims racking their brains as they leave me. They probably want to ask the blessed Mohammed: Why did you, most sacred prophet of Allah, not take a closer look at what Christ has taught? Had you done so, many of the contradictions in the Koran would not exist.

The next day, men are being loaded into prisoner transports once again. Nobody from our barrack has been taken, but every man is keeping his bundled belongings within arm's reach. All the men are nervous. The general anxiety infects our barrack as well.

The Uzbeks no longer come to my lessons.

Soon, some gold-epauletted men enter the barrack with the prison foreman and some camp guards. They call out some names. Mine is not on the list.

In the general confusion, the mullah makes his way toward me, a small bundle clutched in his fingers.

"I'm being taken away on the transport," he says sadly. "I'm sorry that we cannot continue our readings." Then, he brightens, holds up two fingers and declares: "Allah, il-Allah!" And then, he hugs me hard and kisses me, adding: "And you are my Christian brother!"

And so they leave. The other Muslim does not come to say good-bye. Perhaps he was unable to express his true feelings in Russian, and chose to depart silently.

I sit on my bunk for a long time, alone with my thoughts, silent.

I had tried to convert those two Muslims. Perhaps they were trying to do the same to me. Which one of us was proselytizing the other? Perhaps it had been unnecessary by either side, because we had simply enjoyed each other's company. We could have such a wonderfully broad platform of unity and inclusiveness, one on which we could achieve a meeting of minds! Christian and Muslim would be united in love, if they wished it to be so. We might achieve something even greater. I feel that the ultimate goal should be that of coming together, one human being with another, regardless of either one's convictions.

I regret very deeply that I had been unable to tell him that I considered him to be my brother, too.

I had been too embarrassed.

(Magadan Transit Camp, November 1949.)

IS YOUR TOBACCO ANY GOOD?

Tsuruk, the Jewish boy from Poland, made every effort to convince me that his forefathers had been Turkish. Even his surname was proof of that.

It was all the same to me. But he had such Jewish habits that I could have no doubt about his origins.

One day, he was brought into a barrack that was supposed to be a warehouse, but instead housed an "underground" workshop of shoemakers, tailors, a Latvian Air Force Officer who was a sculptor, and me, an artisan. We also slept there. In addition, a well-read old man, the night watchmen's brigade commander, had slipped in with us. The same barrack was also used by the prison camp personnel for liaisons with girls who climbed over the fence separating the women's camp from ours. In other words, it served as an underground brothel too.

We all wondered how the ruddy-faced Pole managed to slip in with us. He was not a specialist in anything. He told us he had been assigned to the post of artisan's assistant. My assistant, in other words. But he had no skills that would make him suitable for this position beyond a talent for chatter. Although he claimed to have graduated from secondary school, it looked like he had never drawn a single figure in his life. Finally, we reached the unanimous conclusion that he had been slipped in there to spy on us. That meant we could not speak as freely as we previously had.

He was a splendid businessman.

He found out where to buy tobacco, and eagerly set about doing business. Tobacco meant bread. You could buy an extra portion of bread for a pinch of tobacco every day. But Tsuruk had no money. I still had 20 rubles that I had received for my good homemade felt boots, which I had been forced to sell. Otherwise, they would have been stolen.

Tsuruk hounded me to lend him ten rubles to buy tobacco. It was good tobacco, and quite a bit of it too. We agreed that both of us would make use of it. But as he chewed the first piece of bread that he had broken from the rations of a fellow sufferer, I was filled with disgust. The thought of taking bread from my brothers repulsed me. We agreed that we would split the tobacco, which had been purchased with my money, in half, and we each would do whatever we wished with our half.

Soon, Tsuruk vanished from our barrack, but my tobacco was still there.

To pass the time, I had started carving wooden toys. People liked them, and some found their way into the hands of the commanders' children. I was transferred from the underground workshop to the prison cabinetmaker's workshop.

It was a pitiful hut with a low ceiling and two tiny windows. A fire burned in the iron stove all day to keep us from freezing to death. In addition to me, two cabinetmakers and a tinsmith worked there, making spoons by hammering them out of strips of metal from discarded cans.

Now, my official job consisted of making toys and all kinds of carvings.

During a roll call, which was usually annoying and time-consuming thanks to the illiteracy of the guards, we were herded into Barrack 6 until they could reconcile all the lists. Barrack 6 was where they kept the criminals who had been sent to Kolyma after the Vorkuta uprising. These hoodlums never let an opportunity slip by. They shoved their way through the prisoners crammed into the barrack. They clambered over the bunks, they crawled under the bunks. The barrack was a bustle of nonstop activity. And they filched every last item of any value from the pockets of the political prisoners.

I talked to a young Austrian who had been studying at the Academy of Art in Vienna, and who, as a prisoner of war, had been placed with men sentenced under Article 58. He had hidden his rations under his quilted jacket. He felt his jacket and suddenly realized that his bread was gone. Who took it and how? My eyes had seen nothing, although I was standing almost chest-to-chest with the Austrian. Fearing the worst, I patted my own jacket pocket. I had sewn a piece of fabric to its lining, making a pocket in which

I always carried my New Testament. Now the pocket was empty. Its bottom had been cut away with a razor. My greatest treasure was gone. Raising a protest in that environment would have made as much sense as passing a sentence on a corpse.

After the roll call was over, I sat very sadly at my workbench and prayed to the heavenly Father to return my bread to me. My prayer gave me a little hope.

Barrack by barrack, the men are already drifting toward the mess tent. After the meal, they all must pass our workshop hut as they return to the barracks.

Anxiously, I wait for the end of the mealtime for Barrack 6. As they exit the mess tent, they are held in an enclosure until they have all assembled. It is here that I approach them and say to the closest man: "Brothers, I lost my valuable book in your barrack during the roll call. Has anyone found it?"

The foulmouthed brutes only sneer at me, trying to outdo each other with creative insults at my expense. I become quite dejected. Then one of the stick-wielding men lets them out of the enclosure. One of the last men out whispers: "Come to our barrack later."

That means my book is still there.

I give my soup away to one of my hungry compatriots. I do not want to eat a single bite until I once again hold my heavenly bread in my hands. I search for something that might convince these thieves to return my book, but I find nothing besides the little bag of tobacco which Tsuruk had purchased to exchange for bread. And now, I would also be exchanging tobacco for bread. Since tobacco was hard to come by, I hoped that I might be successful if I offer it to them.

The attendant who sweeps up wood shavings and wood scraps from our workshop opens the door of Barrack 6 without even demanding a bribe.

I step into the dimly lit room. The white underpants of the men lying on the bunks seem to glimmer. Apparently, they have had another wild card game, and some of the men have lost their clothing. That is their style. First, they bet their rations from the seventh day onward, then their clothes, and finally their lives.

It is hard for a regular person to understand this community and its customs. The camp is almost an inevitable continuation of their danger-filled lives. Even at the camp, they have well-established laws and customs. They divide themselves into two classes – the *sukas* ("bitches", criminal prisoners who collaborate with Soviet authorities) and the *urkas* (the so-called "honest thieves," professional criminals who terrorize the other prisoners), two groups with an ongoing bloody rivalry. It is typical for them to butcher each other without mercy. However, they usually leave the political prisoners, whom they called *muzhiki*[38] or *freiers* (non-thieves, neutrals), alone...unless these prisoners have anything that can be taken or stolen, of course.

And now I stand in the nest of the most disreputable *urkas*. Which one should I turn to first? Which one should I talk to? If they all crowd around me, they might even rip the pants off my body.

As soon as I step in, they become attentive, but not one of them approaches me. I look around beseechingly. On a high bunk, I suddenly spot the old man with the pock-marked face whom I had seen in the dentist's waiting room at the work zone. We had spoken a few words to each other there. And now he is lying up there on the bunk, quilted coat pulled up over his shoulders, staring at me like all the others. I go right up to him, greet him cordially and tell him about the quest that has brought me to their barrack. He listens attentively, and without responding to me in any way, rolls onto his belly and orders hoarsely: "On your feet, all you filthy thieves!"

All the men sit upright. I realize he must be the chieftain of the thieves.

Immediately, two young men rush up to him, awaiting orders.

His orders are brief and clear: "Find the book for *batyushka*!"

Immediately, the adjutants begin their quest. From one end of the barrack to the other, they pat down all their comrades with the skill of true thieves, and a few minutes later they return, holding my beloved spiritual bread in their hands.

"Is this your book?" asks the chief.

"Yes, that's it. I'm so glad you found it."

"What are you going to give us for it?" one of the young thieves asks me.

38 *muzhiki* – Group of men; men in general; peasants

"I brought along a little tobacco for your chief." As I say this, I hold out my little bag, which I had been holding tightly in my hand, to the pock-marked man.

But he says: "Give it to the boys."

And so I hold it out to those fellows.

One of them asks: "Is your tobacco any good?"

"You'll have to see for yourself," I tell them, handing over the bag.

They take a pinch, sniff it and sing its praises as if in chorus: "Good tobacco!"

And then I am given my book.

Only the first page has been torn out and probably smoked.

Maybe the paper had been too thin, or maybe they had nothing to roll into it, but they had destroyed no more of my precious treasure.

Apparently, they had searched me thoroughly as I was busy thanking and blessing them for the return of my book, because the only thing that I had had in my pocket – my handkerchief – was missing.

(Magadan Prison, December 1949)

CHRIST HAS RISEN

"*Batyushka*, come to Barrack 7 today. We're having a Passover service," whispers Aritsko into my ear. He is saying this as if in reconciliation.

Oh, that Demjan Aritsko! He was a memorable individual. I could not figure out what to make of him. After being brought to the special zone, I was placed in Barrack 3, and he made room for me on the bunk next to himself. My first meeting with this western Ukrainian had been quite pleasant. Every morning and every evening, he knelt on his bunk, prayed, and crossed himself reverently. His speech was reasonable and measured, and he rarely swore. But I soon realized that he was conducting some kind of business with the women's camp on the other side of the fence. Sometimes he would leave the fence with a bread ration under his coat. Apparently, he had some kind of business dealings with the women. Thanks to him, I managed to sneak the text of a sermon to some Estonian girls in the women's camp along with some crosses that I sent them as Christmas gifts. I had carved the crosses from old toothbrushes and pieces of combs.

As I awoke one morning, I found that my woolen socks were missing from the bag under my head. I immediately related my misfortune to Demjan. He made a sad face and shrugged broadly. He could not imagine who would do such a horrible thing. Well, the socks were gone. There was nothing I could do. I still have my foot-cloths; I will wrap my feet with them and get by. Two days later, I found that the warm underpants I had brought from home had disappeared. When I told him about it, Demjan again made a sad face and shrugged. He cannot imagine who could be stealing things from my bunk. And then, I happened to hear a whispered conversation between his Ukrainian buddies on the bunk right above mine. They were talking about someone named Marusya who was begging them for more wool yarn. I smelled a rat. My socks were probably being unraveled in the women's camp for someone to knit a sweater or other garment. But they would not have enough yarn for something like that. I had another pair of woolen socks that I was keeping in case I was sent to a camp. I could wear them under my foot-cloths. On the morning after I overheard this discussion, I awoke and found my socks missing. Now I had no more doubts about who was acquiring extra bread rations for himself in exchange for my property. But how could I expose the thieves? That would be rather difficult. Besides, I had nothing left for these Ukrainian thugs to barter with.

One day, the foreman came looking through the barracks for older men to sweep chimneys in the women's camp. I agreed to go immediately. Demjan wanted to go too, but he was excluded as being a bit too young. Who knows what kind of mischief he might get into when his blood, cooled for too long, is suddenly brought to a boil.

I spent an entire day with another old man clambering over the roofs in the women's zone. The work itself was not that hard, since the barrack stoves have no flues to speak of, the kind of flues that a chimney sweep would clean of soot with his crooked-stemmed ladle. I succeeded in talking briefly to the Estonian girls. And they confirmed my suspicions about the Ukrainian girls having some business dealings with the men. One of them was indeed named Marusya.

After I returned home that evening, I noticed Demjan glancing at me furtively from the corner of his eye. He sensed that I suspected him of stealing. Without further ado, I grabbed him by his lapels and said: "Do you want me to beat you up right here, or should I go complain to the regime commander?"

"What, what do you want from me?" stammered Demjan, stunned.

"I want to do what they usually do to any thief in the camps when he's found out," I shout, raising my voice above the din of the barrack.

His compatriots start climbing down off their bunks to Demjan's defense.

"Why are you accusing him?" snorts one little twit, the most nervy of them all.

"Because I saw Marusya with my socks and pants, and she said she had bought them from you."

At that, everyone became silent. Indeed, I had not said a single word to Marusya, but it was evident that my words had hit uncomfortably close to the truth.

"Well, I'm guilty," stammered Demjan suddenly. "Forgive me, and don't go telling anyone." One of his gang members climbed down from his bunk with a bread ration, which he offered to me. It was the ration he had gotten in exchange for the socks.

My heart softened. I left them unpunished, but struck a deal with them. They would give me a mugful of tea and a piece of bread every day until it equaled the amount they themselves had eaten in exchange for my property. They agreed, and our daily life as prisoners of the transit camp returned to normal.

And now Aritsko is inviting me to a Passover service. There is also a Unitarian preacher in our barrack. However, I had not figured out how to connect with him. He was always engrossed in his prayer book, and acted annoyed whenever I approached him. And so I found communion among the Evangelists and Baptists, who always graciously made room for me on the bunk whenever they prayed. I would usually translate something for them from the New Testament, adding a few words in explanation. Soon, they had accepted me as their brother. We were also joined by the Mennonites. When the faithful in the other barracks heard of our blossoming communion, they tried to join us. We were able to meet our brothers during our walks, if nowhere else. All those who survived the terrible hardships and ended up in Seimchan joined our underground congregation after being released from the camp.

But I agree to attend the Catholics' Passover service.

Barrack 7 is crowded with men. Four priests are celebrating the mass. An improvised altar has been constructed of a table covered with blankets. Naturally, they are not of liturgical colors. The iconostasis is drawn by hand, and the cross held by the priest is made of wood. However, it is so heavily covered with lacquer that is shines, as if made of gold. The men sing the choral parts of the liturgy in multiple harmony. It is a joy to hear. And that same little priest who enjoys meditating alone in our barrack walks among the congregation with the cross, which the men kiss reverently, boldly singing the trope: "Christ has risen from the dead; with death He defeats death; He gives life to the faithful in their graves."

Demjan Aritsko stands near me and sings, huge tears rolling down his cheeks. At this moment, I could not call him "the thief Aritsko," but rather refer to him as "sad Demjan." May our resurrected Lord enlighten his heart, so that he will never again be indifferent to whether he is engaging in a religious service or acting in slavery to Satan.

But I can barely start my prayer when the barrack door clanks open and the camp chief steps in with seven guards. All the men see them and face them, as if on command. Only the priest fails to look in their direction. He raises the cross high and repeats "Christ has risen." And oddly enough, the entire congregation continues to sing. The song swells in volume, becoming victorious, even threatening. The chief, trailed by his entourage, walks over to the altar, picks up the prayer book and leafs through it. Now the men fall into an abrupt silence. But this silence is so sinister that the eight epaulette-wearing men whirl around, startled. Without a word, the chief places the book back on the altar, and leaves with a challenging look, his head held high.

The service continues. These words echo victoriously: "Christ has risen from the dead; with death He defeats death..."

It is an unforgettable experience for me. By the end of the service, I am so overcome with emotion that I feel indebted to the priests. I approach them and introduce myself as their Protestant colleague. Although they greet me warmly, they do not want to stay and talk to me. To one of them, I suggest conducting a joint Bible study group for the purpose of mutual improvement of our theological knowledge and spiritual wisdom. But the priest pretends not to hear me. I assume he did not understand, so I turn to another priest with the same suggestion. He only smiles and shakes his head. I am confused. I express my sincere wish to even a third priest. He calls the little priest from our barrack over to listen. As I wait for an answer, he turns to his colleague from our barrack and asks: "What do you think?"

With the deepest modesty, he replies: "We can not pray together with a heretic."

I feel as if someone has dumped a bucket of ice water onto my head. All the reverence I have just experienced during the service is wiped away by an invisible merciless hand. Even in these conditions, in this kind of life, the representatives of the Catholic church hold fast to this madness which should have heard its death knell long ago. Even in the camps, they feel they represent the strict principles of Catholicism, telling everyone that redemption of the soul is not possible outside the Catholic church.

Suddenly, I feel that the four priests who have just celebrated Passover mass are not representatives of Christ's church, but rather of some medieval religious guild which is more than happy to toss anyone with a difference of opinion to a Court of Inquisition.

Perhaps I understand Demjan Aritsko and his gang better now. Although they are conspicuous with their piety, their secret wretchedness is much greater than their faith.

Some time later, it comes as little surprise to me that one of the priests, while serving as a duty officer, was beaten up by the men for stealing someone's bread rations.

Doctor Ivanjuk, with whom we had held communion on the ship, had been a different man altogether.

But the Catholic church has foresight. It had provided Demjan Aritsko with spiritual shepherds who suited him perfectly. For his purposes, those four priests had carried out their duties just as he would have wanted them to.

(Magadan Transit Camp, Winter 1949)

THE LAST DAYS IN THE TRANSIT CAMP

I know quite a bit about manufacturing nails, since I had to spend time at the nail factory at the Magadan Transit Camp. My only problem was that bum of a toolkeeper who kept heaping verbal abuse on me. He claimed he could not keep up with sharpening all the axes that he loaned to me daily. He asked: "Hey, you miserable worm, do you even know how to use an ax?"

"Of course I do, my dear, or I wouldn't keep borrowing them from you."

"You f--- dick, you use the ax for chopping rocks," he says angrily.

"No, I only chop wood," I say, trying to calm him.

After that, he gave me no more axes, and my "nail factory" was forced to cease operations. They had acquired an enormous pile of crates, all constructed with factory-made nails. I now had to pull these nails out and straighten them back up. That took a lot longer than my nail "factory" operations had taken, which went as follows: I would shove the head of the ax, blade up, into the ground, unravel the barbed wire, and place a proper length of it onto the ax blade. A blow with the hammer – and the bit that falls off is now a nail. It lacks a head, but if it is not too long, you can hammer it into wood. And because the carpenter is going to hammer it crooked anyway, a headless nail is really no problem.

Previously, I had chopped nails on a rock, using a chisel. But it took too much time. Besides, the chisel had much less of a sharp surface, and it dulled much more quickly than an ax.

The carpenters now had fewer nails, but the ones they had were genuinely "factory-made." They had no reason to complain. I had little enthusiasm for this work, because I was excited about another project of mine.

The Ukrainians' Passover service had inspired me to serve my countrymen more faithfully with the Word of God. As a member of the carpenters' brigade, I had free access to all the barracks. I wanted to take advantage of this access to do the work of the Kingdom of God. Every day, after I had taken apart a few boxes and straightened about a kilogram of nails, I asked the brigade commander for permission to go and fix some bunks in the barracks. The brigade commander was impressed with my sense of responsibility and good work ethic, and always gave me his blessing to embark on the journey that took me from barrack to barrack. And so I crossed the camp yard, holding my saw, ax and nail-pulling claw under my arm, looking like a proper repairman. After tinkering with a few bunks in the barrack, I would call my Estonian brethren to join me, and I would read to them from the New Testament. I comforted them, admonished them, and joined them in prayer. It was a pleasant diversion in the monotonous life of us transit camp prisoners. They always looked forward to my visits. Sometimes, they might watch me through a barred window as I walked across the camp yard. I could not possibly visit all fourteen barracks every day, but I always remembered which barrack had been the last on my path of missionary work.

Apparently, the Ukrainians' religious service had frightened the camp command to the extent that they now ignored our brief prayer meetings. The chief might have heard about them from some snitch, but nobody showed up to harass me. God had given me the opportunity to spread His good word in this place. I firmly believe that it was a help and a blessing to many people. Unfortunately, this work of tending to human spiritual needs was to end soon, because spring was approaching and prisoner transports were being loaded to take people to the labor camps. All my countrymen, one after another, were taken away.

Soon, even I had outlived my usefulness.

One morning, the entire carpenters' brigade was ordered to prepare for transport. We were not allowed to take anything along.

I left my belongings, along with the blanket that I had received in exchange for the coat I gave Gleb Nikolajevich, on the edge of my bunk and lined up with the rest of the men, who were soon joined by heavily armed guards with bloodhounds. This time, they did not give us several days' worth of rations, as they usually did when they were assembling us for transport. We joyously hoped that we might be taken to the region around Magadan, where it is a good deal warmer than the northern regions where most prisoners were taken.

It was the 25th day of May. The frost was still popping relentlessly as we were ordered to climb into the truck. No tarpaulin to protect us from wind. That must be a sign that we would not be deported far. Indeed, we did not ride far at all. It was only about 10 kilometers from the camp to the airfield. A "Douglas" airplane was waiting for us. Once, I had flown from Tallinn to Kuressaare on this type of airplane. The others would be experiencing flight for the first time. I was the only Estonian to be afforded this luxury. I had worked voluntarily in the carpenters' brigade. Perhaps that is why we were being spared the hardships of the long trips that we had suffered before, freezing for days on end in the back of a truck. Would I have survived?

Barking dogs had accompanied us to the airplane. As the door was shut on their last bark, we were submitted to the barking of the guard. Loudly, he read his warning: "Everyone sits on the floor without moving. Don't even try to look out the window. If anyone turns his head or stands up, I'll shoot."

But I was tall enough to see everything there was to see through the window. I placed my thick gloves, sewed from bits of leather, under my buttocks, and could easily peek at the window from the corner of my eye.

The plane rose, circled Magadan, and headed north. The view from the window was majestic, but for us, the scene signified hopelessness. Snow-covered peaks sparkled in the sunshine. Mountains and more mountains. I could close my eyes and still see nothing but snow-covered mountains. We were being taken somewhere where the snow might never melt. Judging from the sun, we were heading directly due north. The men dozed. The plane's engine roared and rattled so hard that we shook. Sleep tried to overpower me, but I was determined to meet my uncertain fate wide awake. I prayed: "I lift mine eyes unto the hills from whence cometh my help." However, I realized that this was not accurate in my situation, because I was looking down on the hills and I knew that they held nothing but misery and hardship. It was on this trip that I learned to interpret the 121st psalm correctly. Our help does not come from the hills or mountains. When the children of Israel, in their time of need, sought help by looking to the mountains, a pious poet reminded them that there was no use in seeking help from the hills or mountains. Our help comes only from the Lord, who has made heaven and earth.

Thinking these thoughts, I suddenly felt the nearness of God, a feeling so intense that I wanted to raise both my hands high to grasp His blessing.

But I had to sit still.

We had flown well more than two hours when the plane's engines slowed. We were landing. The men woke and raised their heads as if they had been ordered to look out the window. But the guard barked at us so harshly that they slumped back into heaps more miserable than before. Even I no longer dared peek toward the window from the corner of my eye.

Soon, the plane's wheels touched down on the landing strip of tamped, smoothed earth. A few more bumps, and we were there. I wondered if this was the end of our journey, or just a layover.

We were herded out of the plane, twenty-four at a time, toward a thicket. We realized that other planes carrying loads of prisoners had landed too, because about a hundred men were already sitting there. We were also ordered to sit. We had arrived on a plain surrounded by distant mountain ranges. Nobody knew where we were. But it was a pleasant place, because the sun shone warmly and the larks warbled and trilled their sweet songs above the airfield.

Even here, spring was on its way. If they leave us here, our situation will not be so hopeless.

But this was nothing more than a *seimcha*. That means "valley of the sun" in Yakut. At that time, I did not realize that I would be spending the miserable days of my so-called freedom after being released from the camp in this "valley of the sun," days that would differ little from my days in the camps.

(From Magadan to Seimchan.)

WOMEN, CARDS, BOOZE

The first time Nikolai entered the woodworkers' shop one evening, he was as self-conscious as a schoolboy who had to recite an unlearned lesson in front of the whole class. He was a collective farmer's son from somewhere in the heart of Russia. Before being conscripted, he had studied cabinetmaking at an industrial school, and worked about a year in some workshop. Now he, as a loyal Communist Youth, was guarding prisoners.

Because the garrison needed stools, cabinets, shelves and clothes racks, the cabinetmaking master Nikolai Yegorov was sent to our workshop to make these items.

We were to provide him with tools and materials. The cabinetmakers placed the wood up under the ceiling of our workshop to dry. I carefully collected boards from crates that had held explosives. They were the source of the highest-quality material that we could use for making all kinds of things.

During the day, three Latvians, two Ukrainians and one Estonian worked there; three Lithuanians and I had the night shift.

Officially, I was the toolkeeper. Actually, I had to do any job that our superiors could come up with. I had to assist the cabinemakers, sharpen saws and axes, fashion all kinds of handles, unload boards, write out instructions for drivers, wash the office floor and make toys for children in the free workers' settlement.

In a word – a jack-of-all-trades.

Even Nikolai was my responsibility. I had to help him wherever he needed it. He was a kindhearted Russian boy who soon shook off his fear of fascists and began acting like a human being.

On the first night he came to our workshop, we invited him to join us in eating the porridge I had made from the package I received. But the *Komsomol* member refused.

Then I said to him crossly: "You won't eat with us? Well, then I won't give you any tools either."

At that, he picked up a spoon and stuck it into the can that served as our cooking pot.

Eventually, we began to engage in sincere conversations with this soldier.

I let him talk about how he imagined the future would be for him, a Communist Youth. He did not know much except for what had been crammed into his head during propaganda classes. He had little interest in the topic.

One night, I said to him: "Nikolai, do you realize that here, with your bayonet, you are serving a Godless power, while your mother is at home praying for you. How can you reconcile these two things?"

"But how do you know that my mother is praying for me?"

"Because you look like she is!" I tell him cheerfully.

And then he tells me about his mother. He speaks with great respect. He tells me how their village church was demolished, and how all the faithful now have to travel great distances to attend church services. He talks about the icon in his home, where his mother is always praying. His father was killed at the battle of Kerchi in the Great Patriotic War. He also explained that he had left the collective farm because of the unrelenting famine.

One evening, he brought a letter with him. Joyfully, he reported that he had gotten good news from his mother. At the collective farms around his home, they had gotten bread to eat for the first time since the war's end.

"What have they been eating instead?"

"Well, potatoes, turnips and anything else they could grow."

The war had been over for five years, and they were eating bread for the first time.

"Honor to your people, Nikolai, they are very patient," I say.

"Oh, we're used to it," replies Nikolai dismissively.

One night, Nikolai brings another man along to help him. The garrison wants us to make a whole pile of stools as quickly as possible. The other man is not nearly as sincere or guileless as Nikolai. He has served a sentence of several years for some kind of mischief. It is apparent from his whole being that he is made of other stuff.

But he, like Nikolai, is also a Communist Youth.

Whenever we discuss ideological issues, those two are in total agreement, fully convinced that communism has almost been achieved, and is right here, just barely beyond reach.

But I overhear some of their private discussions, which revolve around three primary topics: women, cards, booze.

One night, their chatter fills me with sudden annoyance. I turn to them with this question: "Tell me, you tough guys, do you imagine that there will be women in the future?"

"Yes, there will!" reply the *komsomolets* in unison.

"Will there be cards?"

"Yes, there will!"

"Will there be booze?"

"Yes, there will, of course there will!"

"But then, there can't be any communism."

Dumbfounded, the soldiers stare first at me, then at each other. For a while, they are silent.

Finally, Serjozha says: "*Batya* speaks the truth."

(Lazo, in the winter of 1950)

EVEN NOW, I AM STILL A BLACKCOAT

The new chief of convoy was a two-striper, a young red-cheeked soldier with a *komsomol* badge. He took over the shift from the guards. Five hundred men are waiting for the "evening prayer" that will allow them to start moving. We called the warning we were given each night our "evening prayer": "Do not talk in line, do not look up or to the side, walk in step. Link arms tightly. Any step to the right or left will be regarded as an escape attempt, and the convoy guards will fire without warning." Those are the words to our "evening prayer." It concludes not with "amen," but with the shouted question "Do you understand?" Usually, nobody answers. That infuriates some of those punks, but the others pay no attention to the fact. After the "evening prayer" comes the order "Move!" and the herd of hunched prisoners begins to shuffle onward. Only the irregular white numbers adorning the backs of their jackets and shuffling in rhythm with the men give evidence that this exercise does indeed have a purpose.

But today, they do not start the night shift with the usual "evening prayer." The men wait.

Suddenly, a two-striper points at me and shouts from the foot of the hill: "All right! You, tall guy, come here!" Since I am the tallest in our shift, there is no doubt that he is referring to me.

But how can I leave the line when I know that stepping out would get me shot? All right, let them shoot me if they want to. After all, I have five hundred witnesses who can testify that I did not leave the line of my own accord. Then again, their testimony might be worthless, considering our situation.

When I reach the red-cheeked *Komsomol* member and stand before him, hands behind my back, as required, he begins derisively: "They say that you have served as a blackcoat."

"Even now, I am still a blackcoat," I respond without blinking. I suspect that his derisive manner means he wants something from me. His predecessors must have recommended me as a woodcarver. The skills of a prisoner who might actually be able to do something for him could not be acknowledged with anything but derision.

But the two-striper is unprepared for my response. He stares at me stupidly, as if confused by the approving murmur that arises from the line at my response.

Helpfully, I ask: "Is there anything else?"

He responds by ordering: "Back in line, you miserable worm!"

I bow to him cordially and say: "I thank you," turn on my heel and go back to the line.

Forgetting the "evening prayer," they bark: "Move!" We plod silently up to the mine.

After the mine gates close behind us, five hundred men gather around me. Each one wants to say something appreciative. All around me, I hear statements like "*Batya*, you really let that S.O.B. have it!" The hefty drill operator calls out: "Good for you, *batya*!" This evening, I feel as if that two-striper has given me the gift of a congregation. Many of them had not known I was a man of the cloth. Now they know. And they know something else as well: that they have a blackcoat among them whose heart remains undaunted, even though he has a number sewn onto the back of his shirt. If I had now, at the foot of this mountain, called on these men to push the guardhouse down into the ravine with the armed guards still inside, they would have done so.

This story has a sequel.

The next evening, once the shift has been secured behind the gates, that same two-striper summons me to the guardhouse. He turns to me, saying rather cordially: "You have made some beautiful things."

"How do you know that?"

"I've seen them."

"And so?"

"Make something like that for me."

"I'd be glad to, if you would treat the prisoners better."

"I'll try."

"We'll see."

That is how our conversation ends. That two-striper actually refrained from berating us for several evenings. But then, as he is counting our shift in through the gates, he asks me: "Have you started making anything?"

"Yes, I have!" I have actually started carving a wooden figure of a ballerina, according to his wishes.

The next evening, he has forgotten his promise and curses us in true Russian style. From the foot of the hill, he calls to me: "Well, is it almost done?"

I reply: "Since your conduct has changed, I will stop working on it."

The men laugh. How pitiful that guard and his automatic weapon look next to a ridiculed wretch such as myself. But he does not say a word.

One evening, he reminds me in front of the shift that he still expects me to keep my promise.

"That depends entirely on your conduct." And from that time onward, nobody could complain about that young man's behavior. I now have the support of five hundred men. I finish carving the little figure. After painting it with bright colors, I let him come fetch it. The boy is delighted with it. In his eagerness, he promises to get me anything I want. I ask him to bring me some cheese, because I had seen some on our foreman's sandwich.

"But I have no money," says the two-striper.

I still have 25 rubles, which I give to him to buy the cheese.

"You'll never see your rubles again," say the cabinetmakers.

Well, I guess if my rubles are gone, they are gone. That cheese will not save my life anyway. The incident will become nothing more than another "flower" in the bouquet of my opinion of Soviet man.

Two days pass without any sign of the two-striper, the money, or the cheese.

On the third evening, another soldier returns my 25 rubles and apologizes, saying there is no more cheese in the store.

All right. At any rate, I remember that Young Communist fondly.

(At the castorite mine in Lazo, 1950.)

A KING'S FREEDOM

King, what was your first name? I have forgotten it. Forgive me! But recalling it is unimprotant in this kingdom. You told me you wanted to enter the true Kingdom, and that is why you did not hate, why you did no harm to anyone, not even to those who sentenced you to ten years for loving your country and your people. And yet, you were forced to submit to the will of the slave drivers for only half that long. Your King granted you amnesty. You yourself never played the role of king; you bowed before Him, despite your proud surname.

I never asked how old you were. Your hair was gray. I never noticed it until one day at the baths. In ten days, your hair had not grown enough to reveal its silvery hue, which would have commanded my respect from the start. Nobody at the camp ever asks anyone how he feels, and so you never revealed that you were gravely ill. I thought you were simply tired, tired like me and all the other men being herded through the gates. I do not know if your workday was 14 hours long, like mine. And I do not even remember if you worked above the ground or below it. But I do remember one morning with you.

The night shift was waiting for the convoy guards. Five hundred men sat on the rocky slope, shivering from cold. The shift was long over, but those *komsomolets* were too busy with heaven-knows-what to inconvenience themselves with lining up the prisoners who just completed the night shift.

Five of us Estonian men walked abreast in the crisp Kolyma morning. We were hungry. We shivered in the cold, and sleep tried hard to force itself upon us.

The night shift was always more difficult than the day shift.

Gradually, I got accustomed to it, because I worked the night shift almost all the years of my imprisonment in the camps.

Only King did not look tired. His eyes, always smiling and yet sad, sought something in the mountaintops.

One day, I started to wonder what he was thinking.

"Tell me, what are you dreaming of now?"

"Oh, I'm just looking at those mountainsides," he replied evasively.

"You see them every day. Why are you gazing at them with such longing?"

"You know, it would be so wonderful to climb up there without an armed guard on your tail."

Yes, it would be wonderful indeed. I had never thought of that before. Now the round-topped mountains seemed more interesting to me too. The other men also shook off their exhaustion and raised their eyes as they listened to our conversation. Each man's gaze reflected the same longing, the longing for freedom. Apparently, the longing for freedom swells up in men's hearts only when that freedom has been lost and when regaining freedom has become but a distant dream.

A few weeks later, King was taken out through the camp gates in a box made of rough planks. And still, an armed guard trailed him. Only when he was already covered with several dozen centimeters of gravel did the armed guard leave.

(This is a recollection from the Lazo castorite mine in Kolyma, in thes pring of 1951)

A BARREL LID FOR STYOSSOV'S OLD LADY

The new mine commander Vladimir Semyonovich Styossov had been a Party First Secretary somewhere. They said his geological education had not been nearly as rigorous as his political education.

It was generally known that his monthly wages were 11,000 rubles and that his wife worked as a shift commander in a sorting establishment, earning an additional 4,000 rubles a month. Their daughter was studying at Lomonossov University in Moscow on scholarship.

That meant they were rather well off. But it did not stop them from coveting even more. Old Styossov had his big dog slaughtered like a calf, and he sold the meat to the explosives workers. Everything they needed was made in the mine workshops, meaning that they did not pay anyone a single kopeck for any of it.

As I arrived at work one evening, the brigade commander gave me an assignment: "Haamer, you have to make a barrel lid for Styossov's old lady. Here are the measurements."

Thanks a lot. It will take me at least an hour, and it will not be recorded as work completed. And nobody will say so much as a kind word to me for it. The brigade commander will get a hand-rolled cigarette or a pinch of tobacco in gratitude. And that is all.

Only two of us are at work that night, the Ukrainian "bandit" Antonenko and I. The cabinetmakers have the day off. By morning, we have to make 12 ladders for 3 divisions, so that the miners can climb through the tunnels leading from one level to another in the areas with no elevators.

After cutting the ladder beams with the circular saw, Antonenko starts drilling holes in them. But I start fashioning a lid for Madame Styossov's sauerkraut barrel. The old Ukrainian peasant, with his unshakeable sense of justice, has already told me what he thinks of the Styossovs. But that provides me as little consolation as the act for which he has been sentenced to 25 years. He was declared a *kulak*[39] and sent to Siberia. One day, he sneaked back and burned down his home village. He was put behind bars. Luckily for him, the death penalty had been rescinded in the Soviet land by that time. That is how he ended up in Kolyma to do his penance. It seemed that nothing would succeed in re-educating him. He was ever poised to do something to avenge the injustice. He loved to work. Together, we successfully completed every project our skilled hands undertook.

Engrossed in our work, neither of us notice the distinguished stranger who enters our workshop. Suddenly, he is standing beside me and saying, as if to an old acquaintance: "Well, well, we're working!"

"Hello!" I say, just in case. I have no idea which of my superiors I am dealing with now.

He introduces himself as the chief of the mine. He is interested in seeing how the work in each station of the mine is going. He asks what I am doing, and whether I am a cabinetmaker.

"No, I'm not."

"But you're doing a cabinetmaker's work, I see." He stares at the half-finished barrel lid. Any geezer can figure out how to make something like this, I think to myself.

"I do it out of necessity, since we have nobody better," I reply.

"Where did you learn it?"

"At the camp."

"Who were you as a free man?"

"A pastor."

"How odd! I've lived on this earth for forty eight years, and I've never heard of this kind of profession before!" boasts old Styossov.

39 *kulak* – Farmer; term used to vilify those who would not give away their land to collective farms

"I've heard you're an educated man. If you're interested, pick up an encyclopedia, and you can read more about my profession," I say very politely.

That must have insulted Styossov, because he barks gruffly: "That means you're a blackcoat!"

"Perhaps in your language I'm a blackcoat. That's all right. You see, you did figure out who I am."

"What the f--- do you need this God of yours for?" the pot-bellied man suddenly roars. In the folds of his face, I see more loathsomeness than fat.

"But why do you use foul language if you're an educated man?" I ask, instead of reacting to his shameless attitude.

"That depends on the group one is dealing with at the moment," says the mine chief in way of apology.

"If our group is so worthless that you cannot use decent language with us, then why do you talk to us at all?"

At that, two round and not unintelligent eyes stare at me for some time. He does not say a word. Then he changes the subject, speaking so politely that he begins to address us, the slaves, in the formal style of speech. He does want to demonstrate his good breeding to this dissenter.

"Tell me, please, why were you sentenced to prison?" he asks me abruptly.

Antonenko has stopped drilling and is listening raptly to our conversation.

"I was sentenced because I could not turn black into white."

"Whoever ordered you to do that?"

"You did!"

"What do you mean – we did! We can see the difference between black and white clearly, and we have tremendous respect for those people who can do the same," says Styossov proudly.

"That's the problem. You cannot tell the difference, and you confuse those who would like to tell the difference!"

"That's not true!" the rotund communist disagrees.

"All right. I'll prove it to you right now. Tell me, please, what is the color of this stove?" The stove, which had just yesterday been painted white, stands behind us.

Styossov turns around. Unable to grasp my intention, he asks: "Why should I tell you that?"

“It’s just an experiment.”

“Well, all right, it seems to be white.”

“I didn’t ask what color it seems to be, I asked what color it is.”

“It looks like it’s white!” Styossov is trying to extract himself from the situation.

“I didn’t ask what color it looks like, I asked what color it is.”

At that, he blurts out angrily, forgetting his desire to appear as an educated person: “Well, if that’s the way you want it, let it be white then!”

“You see, I’ve asked you three times what color this stove is. And all three times, your answer was evasive. Why? Look, you are accustomed to answering questions with the barrel of a gun pointed at you. You look into the eyes of the person holding the gun and asking you questions, and you have a sincere desire to agree with the person who holds your fate in his hands. And so you have no opinions of your own. You cannot see white as white or black as black, if your lord and master chooses to see it differently. But we have been raised to regard white as white and black as black. And you see, that is why I have lost my freedom.”

Styossov has listened silently, but his cheeks have reddened in agitation. He glances briefly at Antonenko, who has just picked up an ax and put it within arm’s reach. Then he turns to me once more, as if trying to win me over: “I see you are a smart man. You could be a good communist if you would just forget about this God stuff.”

“I will never be a communist, because I have not seen any communists setting a good example. The communists I have met have been greedy for things and greedy for power; they have been lewd, they have been drunkards, they have had other faults. How could I ever be like them?” I reply, not without some agitation.

“Then you haven’t met a true communist yet,” says Styossov.

“And where can I find this first true communist?” I ask naively.

“Well, you might use me as an example,” boasts the pot-bellied man.

“Use you as an example? You are less of a communist than any of the others.” My blood suddenly begins to boil. I grab the sauerkraut barrel lid from my workbench and, holding it above my head, raise my voice almost to a shout: “I am making this for you. Because of this piece of junk, you are committing a triple crime. This lid is being made for you without a work order – that means you are defrauding the state. You are not paying anything to the person making it – that means you are exploiting a slave. And finally, you are burdening your conscience with it. And you think I should look up to you as an example? Never!"

Fearfully, Styossov backs over to the door, mumbling: "Calm down, calm down, Haamer!" Apparently, he knows my name. He had come specifically to check on me.

"We'll talk another time, another time," he says, trying to calm me with an apologetically raised hand. And he is gone.

Vehemently, Antonenko squeezes his ax handle and says: "If he had run his mouth any longer, I would have chopped his head off."

He would have chopped it indeed. The old man was sure he would never make it to the end of his 25-year sentence anyway.

Perhaps Styossov had seen Antonenko pick up the ax.

(This happened at the Lazo mine in the winter of 1951.)

SHVED GETS TO WORK

Shved was the son of an Ukrainian bartender, and the prototype of a true bandit. Although he was too lazy to work, he managed to support two "wives." Those rosy-cheeked boys satisfied him in every way. In exchange, he would feed them well.

He had been sentenced to the political prisoners' camp under Section 14 of Article 58. That means he had been apprehended while trying to escape from a camp for criminals. Soviet authorities treated such people much less harshly than they treated political prisoners, who were simply shot if they were caught trying to escape. We were treated to the sight of three young Ukrainian political prisoners who had been captured and shot, and then left at the gates of the Canyon until their corpses began to stink. But this exhibit, instead of creating the fear it was intended to create, filled us with hatred and contempt against the red-epauletted executioners.

Shved's escape attempt had been pardoned, and as an example to all the non-political prisoners, had been sent to a political prisoner camp, where he played the role of lord and master.

It took a great deal of effort to get him outside the camp gates. He was assigned to our brigade. Naturally, the brigade commander had to give him an easy job. He became the night watchman for the woodyard. It was the best job anyone could ask for.

Every evening, he let all the duty officers bribe him with tobacco and tea, after which he stretched out in the workshop office, sleeping until the midnight shift. Then he made himself some *chifir,* babbled drunkenly for a while, and then slept and slept until morning.

During this time, the duty officers could steal as much reserve wood as they wanted for heating the offices of their superiors.

And where else were they to get firewood? The mountain slopes were bare, and nobody made any effort to obtain so much as a twig for firewood. But the offices had to be heated. It was little wonder that firewood reserves were disappearing from the woodyard.

I got along with Shved quite well. He never demanded very much whenever I received packages from home. He never complained very much whenever I scrubbed the office floor or scraped the dirt off it with an ax. Instead, he would get off the chairs, climb onto the desk, and continue sleeping soundly. Only once, after he had knocked an inkwell off the desk onto the floor, did he chastise me for not moving it out of his way. I was the one who had to clean the ink off the floor. By scraping at it with an ax, of course.

One night, a scandal nearly erupted. I was ordered to fashion 150 various types of handles by morning. I did not even have time to wipe off the sweat dripping down my nose. The water in our workshop's fire barrel was frozen, but my body was soaked with sweat.

It was time for the midnight shift. The men working in the mountain were relieved. One of them, a hefty, lazy brigade commander's assistant, stopped by the cabinetmakers' workshop looking for Shved. I had nicknamed him "Adjutant," because I always saw him following on Shved's heels. I was certain that he also shared Shved's "women."

I sent him into the office to wake up his friend himself.

Soon, they came back looking for water to make *chifir* with. The water bucket in the workshop was empty. The Lithuanian cabinetmakers had chosen to ignore the lack of water, because the water had to be fetched from a spring trickling from a hillside about one kilometer away. Usually, we did not feel like hauling it from that distance. We used snow to wash off our sweat and to cook our porridge (if there was any to be cooked). Whenever they brought ice to the distribution station, we would grab a few pieces as we returned with our shift. We would then melt it at the camp for tea and soup.

Shved notices that the bucket is empty and orders: "Haamer, go fetch some water."

"Thanks, I don't need any. You can see I'm very busy. Besides, you're ten years younger than I, so you can fetch your water yourself."

I turn my back to them and keep planing as if my life depended on it.

Suddenly I feel a pudgy red hand on my shoulder.

Shved glares at me with a wild stare in his protruding eyes: "You're going to fetch the water!"

"Not a chance!"

It must be the first time in his life that anyone has stood up to him. It was unheard of. Such "dissent" must seem even more shocking to Shved's Adjutant. It meant that his lord and master was being insulted, and by this pitiful foreigner, no less.

Without waiting for a command, he lunges at my throat and starts to strangle me. Both the men together are trying to squeeze the very breath out of me. Two miscreants who are already trembling with the anticipation of getting high on *chifir* want to pave their way to their intoxication with the corpse of a foreign rebel. They come very close to snuffing out my life.

Both the Lithuanian cabinetmakers watch this farce dumbfounded. Suddenly, they realize that things are getting out of hand. Quiet old Slotkus, a Lithuanian peasant with white hair and blue eyes, grabs an ax from the workbench and shouts in his broken Russian: "Leave *batya* alone, or I'll chop off both your heads!"

The younger Lithuanian, Visgaitis, grips his chisel like a knife and approaches threateningly.

This frightens both of the culprits, and they let me collapse onto my wood shavings, where it takes me some time to recover, gasping for air.

The next evening, as I leave the mess tent before my shift, I encounter Shved in the friendliest of moods. He walks up to me and says, without further lead-in: "You can bring me a handful of dried apples, if you still have any."

I give him the handful of apples. He had indeed been "gracious enough" to spare my life.

Soon after that, he was made commander of the miners' brigade. At that post, he had acted more like a pig than a workman. One day, he was taken away from our camp. Later we heard stories that Shved had been shot in some penal colony.

(This all happened in Lazo, in the winter of 1951.)

THE COBBLERS' 750 PERCENT

Over and over, we heard about how Velikorodnyi and his partner had soled 150 pairs of felt boots in one night. Real Stakhanovites[40].

If you do not believe it, you can see their names engraved on a plaque of honor. Read it and weep – the night shift of the cobblers' workshop fulfilled their quota by 750 percent.

"Well, now those asses will be celebrating for months," muttered the cow-faced Belarusan named Belouss from the sawframe. He was jealous of anyone who had it a little better than he did. Whenever anyone received a larger ration, he complained that it was being taken from his share.

He muttered something else to himself and sauntered over to the shift lineup at the gate.

I tied up my "fur" collar with both strings, because the thermometer on the guardhouse wall was already reading a few degrees shy of -50°C. I had to go to work. The valor of those shoemakers almost made me happy; it meant that our men would not be suffering in torn felt boots. I began to respect that young Ukrainian thug, an officer of Bandera's, who usually treated me very rudely. Whenever I would take my high quilted boots to him for repairs – I was the only worker on the night shift from Barrack 4 – he would growl: "I don't do private jobs."

40 *Stakhanovite* – Legendary, celebrated hard worker in communist countries; muscular icon portrayed on billboards and in films

I asked him quite humbly how this could be a private job, because I was not a private citizen. However, he sent me and my quilted boots away, because he had been ordered to accept torn footwear only from the duty officer.

All right. I put on my boots, tied them on with string, and went to the night shift lineup. Out attire was being inspected at the gate.

The regime commander walks past the lineup, making comments about torn pants and coats. When he comes to me, he immediately notices my tattered footwear. I cannot wear felt boots, because they make my feet swell. I try to get by with the quilted boots. And those darned things do not even last two weeks.

Repeated lice-killing roasting treatments tended to weaken the fabric of the quilted coats, which was then used to sew tops for the quilted boots. I had no complaints about the sole, which was cut from the leg of an old felt boot and would last quite a bit longer. But I was at a loss about how to attach those soles to the badly frayed cotton rags with wadded stuffing protruding at every seam.

The regime commander can tell right away that I am having serious problems with my footwear. He asks me dully: "Man, why are your quilted boots so tattered?"

"They are not mine, Mister Chief!"

"Well then, whose are they?"

"They belong to the state."

The men closest to me snort with laughter, but stifle their merriment as the regime commander sends an angry glance in their direction. He turns to me, takes another knowing look at my ragged footwear, and steps wordlessly into the guardhouse.

"What did you say to him?" grunts a curious Belouss, who is slow to grasp just about everything.

"Nothing but the truth," someone answers on my behalf, someone with a better grasp of the joke.

But the incident failed to improve my situation. The duty officer would probably be reprimanded. He, in turn, would blame me for not giving him my torn quilted boots to take to the repair shop. If I went to the cobblers myself, they would turn up their noses at me, refusing even the most generous bribe in exchange for repairs.

The next morning, as we return from our worksite to the camp, the cold has let up a bit. After the inspection ceremony at the gates has been completed, we dart into the zone, buttoning up our pants. My eyes catch the plaque of honor. The names of the cobblers are no longer there. What does this mean? At the barrack, I ask the duty officer about it.

He says: "Their foolishness is going to cost them dearly. The KBT chief even gave them some vodka for their achievement. Oh, damn, just think of it – they got a nice swig of pure spirits."

Caught up in the excitement of thinking about a nice shot of vodka and jealousy of the cobblers who had received this blessed reward, he neglects to elucidate me further,

I prod: "But why were they given vodka?"

He replies: "Don't you know? Those bums cheated. Cheated in the most dirty way. After one of them had cut out the soles, the other dipped the soles in water, slapped them onto the boots, and set them outside the door. Jack Frost did the rest. They soled 20 pairs an hour that way. They did that with 150 pairs. They could have done even more, but they ran out of boots. The next day, after the workmen returned from their shift, they set their boots aside to dry. And the soles dried right off. I picked a few pairs up off the racks myself. The boot tops came right off, and the soles stayed behind on the rack. And now the party is over for those *sukas*. They are sitting in the isolation cell. And to think that they got some booze for being deceitful!"

"But those felt boots held together for a whole day, with their soles frozen on. That warrants some serious discussion," I say.

"Oh, so you think that they should present this as an innovation and be rewarded for it. That may earn them another shot of vodka. It'll never happen!" The duty officer has talked himself into a rage.

"Of course it'll never happen. Any idiot can see they were being deceitful, but you're the one saying they were innovative, yes indeed, f---ing innovators."

He wants to slug me, even though I am not the one who said those guys were innovative. I do not dare ask him to take my quilted boots to be repaired. Who knows – perhaps all the cobblers are out of business. Maybe the day shift has been taken away as well. Maybe the regime commander will remind the duty officer that he has a man in his barrack with shabby footwear.

And if he does not, maybe my boots will hold together on their own for a couple more days.

(Lazo, in the winter of 1951)

HAAMER, BE A HUMAN BEING!

"Haamer, the auditors are poking around in our rooms."

"Let them poke around."

"But is everything in order?"

"Should be."

"What about support beams?"

"We've got plenty."

"What if there are less in the stack than what the documents show?"

"How could that be? We have about 100 cubic meters surplus."

"Haamer, you're going to get me hanged."

I was astonished. How can he worry about being hanged when we are dealing with a surplus?

Captain Kovalyov barks angrily: "You're sitting here in the office like a fat toad and you neglect to tell me that we have so much surplus."

"But I thought it was a good thing for us to be in the black."

"Oh, you highly educated dimwit! Don't you know that a surplus is worse than a shortage? For a shortage, they'll transfer you to another position. If there's a surplus, they'll hang you."

Indeed, I did not know that.

This retired captain is my superior. Of course he knows best. I am a simple prisoner with no idea how to save him from the gallows.

The auditors do not come to measure the woodpile that day. The camp commander comes by, though, asking us to sell the camp a truckload of firewood, because there is no place else to get any.

Every morning and every night, the prisoners would haul any wood that they found by the mines into the camp. Miners gouged pieces of shattered support beams from cracks between the rocks. The men at the sawmill and the cabinetmakers' shop swept up wood slivers and shavings. Some broke apart explosives crates, since those boards made good firestarters. In short, anything that could possibly be stuffed into a stove was hoarded by the shift workers hoping for even a little heat in the barracks.

Apparently, even the garrison suffered from a firewood shortage. The red-epauletted men solved their problem the easy way. They let the prisoners haul their bits of firewood to the gates. There, the prisoners were ordered to put down every last twig. Then they were quickly herded back into the zone. Later, a garrison horseman would come by and gather up these piles of firewood. Now the soldiers would have warm quarters in which to play dominoes. But the prisoners who had taken great pains to haul this wood down to the camp would be freezing in their bunks.

After the prisoners had been relieved of their firewood at the gate several times, they started hiding it under their coats. We wanted to sneak it in as contraband material. But the *chekists* soon discovered our deceit, and the loot was theirs once again.

We stopped trying. The soldiers were afraid to go searching for firewood at the mines, and we refused to haul it down anymore. Now, everyone was cold.

Finally, there was not even enough firewood to prepare our meals. The camp commander came to the mines looking for help.

The captain orders me to sell five cubic meters of wood to the camp.

But what kind of wood should I sell him? We have nothing but support beams, which cost 175 rubles, 28 kopecks per cubic meter. Regular firewood is more than three times cheaper. But our woodyard is not designated for firewood storage. The firewood shed stands in the free workers' village.

It is not our business to know how Anashev, the woodshed manager, manages to fulfill his plan. The woodshed in the free workers' village was supposed to supply firewood to the camp as well as the mine. Only God knows where that drunkard of a woodshed manager had squandered his firewood reserves. And now, everyone was cold.

But I had been ordered to sell the camp some wood. And I did. A truckload of support beams roared toward the camp, and I presented a copy of the invoice to the camp commander for his signature. Of course, he slipped the invoice into his pocket with a smile, without checking to see what the transaction had cost.

I sensed that the smile would be wiped off his face as soon as he handed the invoice to the chief bookkeeper at headquarters.

The next day, the camp foreman bursts into the woodshed office saying: "Haamer, be a good man and get rid of that invoice for the sale of wood to the camp."

"Why?" I ask, wide-eyed.

"Do you know that the camp commander has to pay the difference between firewood and construction lumber from his own pocket?"

"And what kind of amount is he whining about?"

"He is going to be socked with about 600 rubles."

"I can tell you the exact amount. He will have to pay 616 rubles and 40 kopecks from his own pocket. And tell me – so what? Doesn't he get paid well? If I were a free man, I would pay even more if it would help these miserable prisoners, who have to work hard for their paltry rations and then freeze in their barracks."

"But he does take care of the camp," persists the foreman.

"You worry about yourself and your brethren in suffering, and let that gold-epauletted man worry about himself. Are you some kind of advocate for him? Go back to the camp and leave me alone."

The half-Jew mumbles some obscenities and slinks back toward the mine gates, where a guard is waiting to drive him back to the camp.

Toadies such as this foreman grated on my soul.

After the foreman leaves, the camp commander himself shows up. His brown eyes blaze. He peers into each corner of the office, as if making sure that there are no invisible snitches listening. "Haamer, be a human being and get rid of that stupid invoice. Do you have any idea what kind of a fool you've made of me? You are making me pay more than six hundred rubles out of my own pocket. I have a wife and children. Think about that!"

"I have a wife and children too," I reply, "and none of you seem to think about that."

"Well, that's the way things are. You had some bad luck. But you'll be released, and you'll see them again. You'll go back to work. Your usual life will go on."

This camp commander was nicknamed "Gypsy." Everything about him gave honor to that name.

"Thank you for trying to console me, but if I do what you're asking me to do, I will not be released as soon as I would like. They will extend my sentence for defrauding the state. And I doubt that you would be willing to serve as my defender."

"Of course it's not right, but nobody will ever know about it. In God's name, I won't tell anyone," swears the Gypsy.

"Are you a religious man? You are swearing in God's name."

"No, I'm a communist, and therefore I'm not allowed to be religious. But it is not forbidden to swear that way. I know you are a priest. But that's all right. You are a fine and honest man."

"But I won't be an honest man any longer if I agree to commit fraud."

"You'll still be the same. You won't be taking anything from anyone's pocket. Quite the opposite – you will be doing a good deed by helping someone out of a jam," persists the Gypsy.

"No, I won't do it. I won't be extending my sentence because of your troubles," I mutter, my mood darkening.

"What do you mean, Haamer? Please be a human being. I will not forget any good deed that you do for me," pleads the camp commander.

"No. I will not tear up the report. The invoice has already been stitched into the accounting book." Having said that, I get up to indicate that this conversation is over.

"Haamer, you're a resident of the camp yourself. You will be doing nothing more than a good deed for the camp," says the Gypsy, refusing to back off. It would be easy for me to refute that statement. I have no interest in haggling with him any longer. The camp commander gets up with a sigh and walks down the hill, his shoulders hunched.

As he passes the woodyard, he stops for a moment. He must be looking at those two-and-a-half meter timbers that are squeezing 616 rubles and 40 kopecks from his pocket.

I am thinking of those timbers too. They comprise the surplus of the woodshed. Two communists are now feeling oppressed by that wood. One is being threatened with hanging, and the other may have to do without a few liters of booze.

And what about me? What do I care about them? And the camp?

And yet... Perhaps these timbers will help me buy some favor for my brothers. After all, the Gypsy's demeanor is now more forlorn than ever.

I reconsider. I rip the invoice from the accounting book and run after the camp commander.

"Here, here is your invoice. Do what you will with it."

The Gypsy looks as if he wants to jump for joy. His brown eyes sparkle. He might almost have hugged me.

"Haamer, you are a real human being. I knew it. And I want to do something for you."

"Well, what could you possibly do for me?" I ask doubtfully.

"I will mail a letter for you. All you have to do is write it. I'll come fetch it myself."

"Thank you. I will certainly take advantage of that offer."

The camp commander extends his hand and clasps mine tightly.

He actually did come by to fetch my letter. We were only allowed to write two letters a year. Only rarely did a free man dare to mail a prisoner's letters in the village. Occasionally, someone would ride to Seimchan and mail the letter there.

I do not know whether the camp commander mailed the letter personally, but my family did indeed receive it. He was a human being too.

(Lazo, 1952.)

THE MINE IS OPERATING ON A SURPLUS

Ivan Ivanovich Kun was released. He worked as the construction department's accountant while serving his 10-year sentence. He was very good at recording benefits for himself at the expense of the working men. A Volga German by nationality, he had little respect for his mother tongue. When I spoke to him in German, he answered in Russian. But he was pedantic and conceited, like any true German. He trembled in his boots before any kind of superior, although he had been a lieutenant in the Great Patriotic War, with which he earned himself ten wonderful years in a special-regime camp. He dreamed of being released, seeing his wife again, and restoring his status in the Party. But he was willing to deceive a simple man without batting an eye, just like any *pridurka* (trusty).

He recorded the jobs that I had completed into his own record, to benefit himself and his cronies, but was always willing to accept a payoff from any packages I received from home.

And yet, I cannot say he was ever impolite or crude. Upon arriving at work, he would change his shoes. His quilted coat was backstitched at the waist. Whenever he planned to conduct some shady business at the expense of the cabinetmakers, he would send the brigade commander to do his dirty work.

That brigade commander managed to pull off the most outrageous transactions. Without batting an eye, he would haul a whole truckload of furniture into the free workers' village, and then use the money he made from the sale to eat and drink together with his cronies.

All the cabinetmakers had to do was to keep making new furniture.

Brigade commander Avagimyan, who was simply called Semyon because of his convoluted Armenian first name, claimed to be the son of an Armenian priest. Indeed, that was hard to believe. I would rather have assumed he was the son of a horse dealer or highway robber. He was released at almost the same time as Ivan Ivanovich.

A Ukrainian schoolboy, Mikhail Skolik, who had fought as a Bandera partisan, was promoted to brigade commander. He assigned his countryman Anatoli Stepanyuk to work in the office. Anatoli was also a schoolboy who had supported Bandera; he recited Taras Shevchenko's poetry by heart, and spoke Russian with great revulsion.

But the Ukrainian hegemony in the construction shop did not last very long. During a search, a homemade pistol was found under the floorboards of the woodyard's guardhouse. The Caucasian who had just been assigned to that post as a guard earnestly assured everyone that he knew nothing about the weapon. He was not under suspicion for very long. Hand grenades fashioned from food cans were soon found in the mine passageways.

Security personnel sensed preparations for a revolt. Undoubtedly, some snitches had played a role in informing the red-epauletted men. Extensive searches were launched. The authorities blamed the Bandera supporters, who were then mercilessly thrown into isolation cells. Anatoli Stepanyuk had worked in the guardhouse before the Caucasian; the pistol probably belonged to him. Even he was thrown into the isolation cell for an extended fast.

The Ukrainian brigade commander was replaced by the Belarusan air force officer Ivan Ivanovich Ivaschenko, who had been shot down by the Germans as he was in his fighter giving cover to the squadron of bombers raining death onto Petseri, a city in Estonia.

He came to us from the mountains with his carpenters' brigade, including his inseparable friend, the young man from Setu, Aleksei Lill, whom he particularly admired. As a member of the Self-Defense Organization, Lill had been assigned to guard the crashed plane. There, the Setu boy's heart had softened upon seeing the wounded and miserable Russian pilot. He had gone into the village to fetch a bottle of moonshine. And the pilot could never forget the gesture. Soviet authorities were now letting the Soviet pilot return the favor, placing the two into the same camp and the same brigade. Both were serving 25-year sentences...one for being captured, and the other for doing the capturing.

And now their brigade was being merged with the cabinetmakers' and sawmill workers' group.

I was still working as the toolkeeper, still planing handles for shovels and pickaxes, cutting boards on the saw frame, and unloading loads of lumber at night.

From the remnants of two brigades, we formed a new brigade of forty-two men. It was hard enough to find enough work at this mine. The miners themselves had been crammed together into multi-purpose brigades, even doing most of the carpentry work required in the mine passages.

The new brigade commander was worried. His group no longer included anyone with writing skills. And so they dragged me into the office.

It felt odd to sit at a table and be an office rat once again, after all these years. It was also hard for the workshop and sawmill men to get used to it. Some were jealous, some were glad.

For me, it was a new world. All I knew of this office work was the slogan making the rounds in the camp: "Things happen, and the office writes it up." And now I was the man who had to make things happen. I had to make things happen so that 42 men could get decent rations, that each man could have a decent day's work recorded for each day. But the brigade commander, as well as his assistant, would not be satisfied with less than two days' work recorded for each day.

Forty men were looking to me. I had to figure out what I could do.

Ivan Ivanovich Kun knew what he was doing. He recorded his workers' hours to his own register, and told anyone who complained to go to hell. Should I continue his tradition?

No, and again no. I was all too well aware how this German lowlife had exploited me. I would not become like him. I had to preserve the honor of my people. And furthermore – I am a Christian. I was proud that my conscience had not yet withered. I felt a strong passion to do something that would help my fellow sufferers, despite the fact that they included such cow-faced louts like that Belarusan Dyunin, who had been all too eager to tattle on me when we worked at the sawmill. Or like the "poet"

Rudolf Maksimov, a husky young man, who dedicated a poem to me, but then turned around and contentedly let me do all the sawing work myself, although he was supposed to be my partner. He spent this time looking for his friends in the mine and flirting with the girls in the office.

If possible, I will do something to help even them. But how?

I have two more days until the work summaries must be completed. I remind the brigade commander of this fact. He had given me some papers listing work orders and the volume of work expected with each assignment.

I sit down and start calculating. For ten men, I can assign a 100% workload. But we have 42 men, and each one wants at least a 126% workload, which allows him to earn an extra half day for each day that he actually works.

I am unhappy. I approach the brigade commander.

"This is not enough work, Ivan. There is only enough for 10 men to do 100 percent." But the brigade commander has his mind on other things. He barks: "If you can't do your office work properly, go back to the workshop."

"Right away, Ivan!" I agree. I leave my papers lying where I left them, and go looking for my woodworkers' tools.

I work at my old, familiar job for a few hours. Then, the brigade commander appears and drags me away from my wood shavings and back to the office by my hair. He has laid some summaries of previously completed jobs on my desk. These will guarantee about ten days of normal rations for a couple more men.

"Not enough!" I whine pathetically.

Ivan is enraged. "You are a university-educated man, and all your knowledge has made your head go bald, and now you're annoying me with this kind of shit. Make something up and write it down!" he shouts.

"But, my dear, how can I make something up? How have the others made it up? You must have pity on me."

Ivan says: "The shaft is dark, and that is where you'll find everything you're missing. I have nothing else to say to you."

After imparting that bit of wisdom, he leaves. I still have two days' time. As the workday is ending, the minemaster comes looking for the brigade commander. He leaves a work order in the office. The shaft latrines need repairing.

I cannot imagine who would have destroyed them. Just last year, I had built four myself. Prior to that, there had not been any at all. The regulations require the availability of latrines, and since they had been dreading the arrival of inspectors, the latrines had to be installed. How much they were used is a different story, because the shaft is dark, and everyone simply lets down their pants wherever they feel the need.

Since the brigade commander is not there, I send an Estonian carpenter to see what repairs needed to be done at the latrines. Just in case, he takes along nail pullers, an ax, a couple of boards and a pocketful of nails we had pounded from barbed wire. (Factory-made nails are a rarity.) In an hour or so, my compatriot comes back.

"Did you go up there?"

"Yes, I did."

"What did you accomplish?"

"One of the doors was hanging a bit crooked. I fixed it."

"That's all? Did you look at all of them?"

"Every last one."

The minemaster had apparently passed that one and seen the door hanging crooked. What a mess! It must be fixed!

My countryman had made short work of it. He pounded four or five nails into a strip of automobile tire, and the door hung even once again.

But what should I write up? One hour for a Category 3 worker, including the time it took to climb up and climb down?

I sit at the desk with the work order and rack my brain, with excellent results. I manage to expand this job so that it lasts nine days on paper. I might have spread it out even more if I had not been afraid of exaggerating too much.

The outcome of my efforts is a full job report entitled: "Repair of Latrines in the Mine Shaft." First, one and a half cubic meters of lumber had been hauled to the sawmill from a distance of one hundred meters. Of that, 1.25 cubic meters were sawed into boards of varying thickness. Naturally, all splinters and sawdust were cleaned up. Then, the boards were carried to an elevation of half a kilometer, up a hill with a 60 degree slope. The boards were distributed to three levels. Finally, the boards were nailed to the walls.

For that, we had to fashion 5 kilos of nails. The daily quota was two and a half kilos. The doors were fit into the openings, at a quota of two doors per day. This was considered a Category 4 job. Travel through the mine passages added several kilometers.

Excitedly, I write it all down, make my calculations and keep adding additional jobs.

I had now learned the job of the technical overseer. All my men were receiving 136 percent rations by the end of the first ten-day period, and their workday count added up quickly.

The brigade commander and his assistant received 152 percent rations. In solidarity with the workers, I wrote up 136 percent for myself,.

Suddenly, my nationality became highly respected, and nobody any longer thought that I, as a man of the cloth, was good for nothing more than swinging a censer.

The mine was operating on a surplus.

The mine chief was given a bonus of 10,000 rubles in addition to his salary of 11,000. The chief economist received 4,000 rubles. But I, in the hours after my workday as an office worker, had to make him a potato crate to ensure that he would keep looking the other way.

(At the Lazo mine in Kolyma, 1952.)

I ELIMINATE THE SURPLUS

"Haamer, the situation is critical. They might be coming to the woodyard tomorrow!"

"Who?"

"You know, the auditors."

"So what?"

"Then I'll be hanged."

That retired captain must have hanged a few people himself to be so afraid of hanging.

I must have stared at him so stupidly that he became agitated.

"We have to do something, Haamer. Think of something."

What could I possibly think of?

"We could cover the lumber with snow. Then you can't see it as well."

"But this committee includes a f---ing mine surveyor. He'll dig the entire woodpile out from under the snow. We have to think of something better."

I go to the workshop and ask the advice of my Lithuanian brothers.

They shrug their shoulders, and none of us can think of a better solution. We try to figure out how the surplus got into our woodyard in the first place.

When the truck driver picks up his load in the forest, the truck is loaded by prisoners. They always leave the last few timbers unloaded. This saves them the expenditure of a few calories. And it is a sure thing that the truck driver, as he passes his own home with the load, tosses a few logs off his load by the front door of his own hut. His wife wants to be warm too.

By the time he drives into the woodyard, his load is significantly smaller than it should be. When I first started receiving the logs, I would measure the load and admonish the truck driver for the half cubic meter that was missing. I should have filed a report, as my bosses had ordered. Later, just looking over the load, I could tell that there were fewer logs than were indicated in the paperwork. But I made out the receipts according to what was marked on the invoice.

One morning, my boss discovered my deceit.

He was there before the shift began. A load of support timbers was just pulling into the yard.

"Do you check the loads?" he asks doubtfully, ignoring my "Good morning."

"Of course I check them," I say with false self-assurance.

"Well, go out and check how many logs there are in that load."

I go out with my measuring stick.

The driver was the old thief Bykov, who never stole less than a whole cubic meter from every load. This time, he was missing one and a half cubic meters.

We wrote up a report. A grumbling Bykov signed it, as did the boss. Since I was the writer of the report, I signed it too.

At the end of the month, I have to send the report summary, along with other documents pertaining to transactions in the woodyard and cabinetmakers' workshop, to the mine's chief economist. And then, 262 rubles and 82 kopecks will be deducted from Bykov's salary for the missing load.

Each time he drives in with a new load, that poor man implores me to destroy the report. But I refuse.

"Our boss ordered me to make the report. Talk to him. It's not my business. I don't want any years added to my sentence because of you, you swindler."

He does go and talk to the boss.

A few days before the end of the month, the retired captain demands that I give him the report. I rip it out of the notebook. When I submit the monthly report summary to the mine office, it does not include this report.

Once, I asked Bykov how much this favor had cost him.

He cursed and said he had to buy the boss 500 grams of booze.

That was not a lot. The value of the stolen property was more than a hundred times that.

Despite all this, we still had a surplus. When the Caucasian had worked as the gatekeeper of the woodyard, he too had been diligent in getting rid of these surpluses, because he would give every duty officer as much firewood as he could carry, in exchange for a pinch of cheap tobacco or one "Belomor."

But the surplus kept growing and growing. It happened like this. Every day, the miners brought us their minemaster's or division chief's orders to distribute so and so many cubic meters of support timbers. Before I came to realize what "great enthusiasm" the miners had for their work, I always recorded the number of logs distributed as greater than the number that was actually handed out, to cover the deficiencies caused by the chronically inadequate truckloads. Later, I would add a few extra logs to the miners' pile.

The prisoners had to carry these logs up the hill on their backs. It was difficult, brutal work. When the men had carried away half or a little more than half of the logs, and realized that their energy was flagging, they would simply return the rest of the logs to the woodpile. If they needed more support beams in the mine passages, new orders would be written out. And no one in the mine passages bothered checking to see whether or not they had been delivered the amount of lumber requested. Also, some of the beams were demolished during explosives work, and the pieces were hauled away to mine offices, the smithy, the mechanical workshop, drill repair shop, distribution center, and even to the prison zone for heating purposes. And in the woodyard, the surplus stubbornly kept growing.

How could I get rid of the extra wood? After all, why shouldn't all those bosses be hanged? They had come here to Kolyma to earn truckloads of rubles knowing full well that they would do so from the sweat and toil of slaves. And now he wants a slave to save his neck from the noose. Thanks a lot!

Suddenly, Slotkus remembers something. "Maybe the woodyard in the free workers' village has a deficit. You could get a document from them stating that they have sold you a quantity of wood that equals our surplus."

"That's a good idea. Let's see if it works." I wipe the dust off my pants and return to the office. At the door, I meet the foreman. He is a job supervisor from Minsk who has served time in the thieves' camp. He is a tall, gaunt man who speaks very little and whose face shines with kindness only if someone is treating him to 100 grams of vodka.

"Chief, I have to talk to you. Please step in for a minute."

Wordlessly, the tall Sotnikov steps in.

"You've got it nice and warm in here," he says, going over to the stove to warm his fingers.

I explain our problem to him, and ask him to if he would go to the free workers' village and get an invoice from Akashev for one hundred cubic meters of lumber which he could claim to have sold us.

Sotnikov says: "That would be a good idea indeed. Akashev has some tremendous shortages. He doesn't have a single twig left in his woodyard. That means he could easily have given them all to you. But he had only firewood, whereas you have strong support beams."

I reply: "It is only important that he gives us the invoice. We'll take care of everything else."

That was the extent of our conversation. The following day, neither the auditors nor Sotnikov showed up. I told the Caucasian at the gate that I would like to discuss the matter with the duty officer myself. When the men arrived, each with their pinch of tobacco, I ordered them to carry away as much lumber as they could possibly carry that night. "If each of you rats doesn't carry off at least two cubic meters overnight, you'll never get so much as a twig, ever again."

I have to give them credit – they were terribly hard-working that night. If only the boss could have seen how well I was liquidating his surplus!

When he saw me the next morning, he asked: "Well, how are things going?"

"Everything's fine," I reply.

"Well, you'd better watch out!"

The third day came, and no auditors appeared. But then, Sotnikov stumbled into the cabinetmakers' workshop. He had been as drunk as a lord for three days. Akashev had treated him well after the recent transaction.

With an elegant gesture, he slaps the invoice for the sale of one hundred cubic meters of lumber onto the table and jabbers: "Be happy, Haamer! I saved your neck from the noose!"

Those prisoners – the ones who have been released – are wonderful guys. In no time at all, they have become just like their lords and masters.

At any rate, he was drunk enough to not be insulted when I picked up the invoice without thanking him.

(Lazo, in the winter of 1952.)

BERIA HAUNTS US

"Nikolai Ivanovich, let me stay behind to guard the factory!"

"You're trying to get out of attending the demonstration again," says the factory boss in response to my request. But he turns around, wishes everyone a good holiday vacation, and does not mention the guard assignment to anyone else.

That is how I, a prisoner who has served his sentence, avoided demonstrating my loyalty to the state for a second time. I spent the October Revolution holiday in the tidy workshop, reading and napping. It was so wonderfully quiet. I could think my thoughts peacefully for hours on end, and tell my God what I was feeling. Nikolai Ivanovich came into the factory only once to check if I was actually on guard duty. His eyes were like slits, his nose red, and his gait unsteady. Apparently he had been celebrating the holiday with gusto, and yet he was no more talkative than usual. He mumbled a few sentences to "console" me for my "state of abandonment" and went off again.

Now it was time for May Day celebrations. In Kolyma, it was still the dead of winter. But the workers had to go outside with their banners, painted with apple blossoms and daffodils. They had to march in the -30°C chill, yelling "hurrah!" and prancing around in their felt boots.

I had to help prepare for this demonstration.

One day, our bookkeeper brings an armload of pictures of the communist saints down from some corner of the attic, spreads them out across my workbench and says: "Haamer, here's a little job for you."

I have to make frames for the pictures and attach them to poles.

Soon after that, the warehouse keeper slaps a bucket of red paint onto my workbench. I must also paint the frames and poles.

On the last day of April, at the end of that ten-day period, I was paid 41 rubles and 60 kopecks for constructing and painting 13 frames to be held aloft on poles. That was the last time that anyone showed any interest in them. I relegated the poles and frames to a corner of the workshop, where they stood like a gaggle of miserable sinners awaiting their fate.

The morning of May 1. A snowdrift has appeared at the edge of the lumber pile in the workshop yard overnight. Powdery white snow blows gently off the snowdrift.

The bell rings at the gate. I pull down the earflaps of my hat and rush outside with my keys to open the gate to our yard.

Our machine factory people and female office workers have arrived, their noses red with the cold. They have assembled here to attend the demonstration together.

Since the cabinetmakers have locked up all their tools, I let this small army come inside.

The personnel director, a primped and painted 40-something Jewish woman, appears to be the organizer of this group. As soon as everyone is inside, she demands, rolling her r's: "Where are the portraits?"

Nikolai Ivanovich has helpfully grabbed all the Russian gods into his arms and placed them onto my workbench. Comrade Burmistrova grabs them one at a time and hands each one to the demonstrator standing closest to her. This person must carry the portrait in the procession.

Suddenly, she recoils. She holds a red frame and pole in her hands for some time before she can compose herself enough to shriek: "What kind of nonsense is this?" Her voice is a croak. Nikolai Ivanovich darts to her side to see what the problem is.

Whenever our factory boss becomes agitated, he begins to stutter. Even now, he shouts in bitter rage: "Who d-d-did th-th-th-this?"

"Haamer," mumbles Belorus, who shies away from any kind of unpleasantness, even if it does not pose any direct threat to him.

"And where is this Haamer?" screeches the painted lady.

Before anyone can point me out, I step up to her, jangling my keys.

"What's wrong?" I ask, my expression uncomprehending. "Is the frame defective, or hasn't the paint had a chance to dry?"

Without replying to my question, the enraged personnel manager shouts: "Who have you put up on this pole? Who are you expecting us to take out there? See for yourself. Look whose name is on the picture." With this, she shoves the banner under my nose.

I read the name, emphasizing each letter: "Beria."

"Beria! Of course it's Beria!" The enraged woman's voice is now almost a shriek.

"His picture was there with all the others. I assumed he was as fine a man as all the rest," I explain, quite apologetically.

"Idiot!" thunders Burmistrova, throwing this fallen Russian god into the corner with a crash, breaking the frame I had made with such loving care.

The rest of the faces are all deemed acceptable. Their demise is still to come. And they are carried out into the blizzard.

After my guard duty, I am given three days off. This time, I was lucky.

When I return to work, Nikolai Ivanovich calls me in to talk about the Beria affair. He begins: "Listen, you played dumb awfully well. Otherwise, that situation may have cost us dearly."

"What do you mean – I played dumb? You considered Beria to be a great man. He imprisoned many, many people like myself, and we all worked for many long years without pay. He helped to build the Soviet state better than anyone else. How could he possibly not be a good man?" I say in self-defense.

"All right, fine. I know you're not as stupid as you pretend to be. But next time, that kind of sarcasm will cost you dearly," states Nikolai Ivanovich, and that is the end of our conversation.

Our duty officer, an old Orthodox Ukrainian, is overcome by such a rush of enthusiasm that he burns the portrait of Beria, along with the frame and pole that I had shellacked. I cannot understand how the fruits of my labors, framing the face of that ape, have suddenly become so worthless that nobody wants to keep them around.

(In Seimchan, May 1, 1955.)

THE JOURNEY HOME

In the spring of 1954, I was taken by a released prisoners' transport to the town of Nizhny-Seymchan, where I became a woodturner and cabinetmaker in the woodworking shop. I had learned the trade of woodturner in the camps.

There were many Estonians in Seymchan, but because they considered themselves to be nearly "home free," they cared little about God. Only during the holidays were they willing to hear me as we sang a few hymns together and became serious in prayer.

One young man who had been with me at the camp attained living faith by reading my New Testament. He lived with a devout Russian brother in whose home other brothers gathered to read the Bible. Soon, I was also a member of their "congregation." It was governed by genuine consensus, and when we started planning to build a church in Seymchan, it would have been difficult to decide which denomination would be represented there.

Simply talking about a new church was so exciting that many outside people began offering their help for its construction. However, the idea never came to fruition, because my "lifelong" exile came to a surprising end.

Little girls would come to my cabinetmaking workshop to watch me work. I turned toys for the kindergarten on my lathe. The girls pleaded, "Uncle, make us some toys like that too!" "Choose the ones you like," I replied. They selected some toys and scampered away. A short time later, they reappeared at my lathe. Again, I had to satisfy their requests.

As I usually did on the first of the month, I went to register myself with the security chief to let him know I was still around. This time, a little girl ran into the office and whispered something into the special commander's ear. That little girl was one of my "customers." After she scampered off, the special commander turned to me and said, "Stay here after the others have gone."

I stayed. "Why were you arrested?" he asked. "You have my files; take a look and see what they say," I replied. He found my file on the shelf, and after perusing it for some time, began swearing in Russian. "Is something amiss with my files?" I asked. He replied, "They jailed you on the basis of sections of the law that the court did not even accuse you of violating!" "How, then, did these sections of the law make their way into my files?" In response, he only uttered a few obscenities and reassured me by saying that he would send my files to Magadan for review.

Six months later, he summoned me, extended his hand and said, "Congratulations! You were arrested by mistake! Now you will be given a passport and you can go wherever you want!"

Just at that time, God gave me an extraordinary opportunity to earn money for my long journey home. From early morning to the late nighttime hours, I stood at the lathe and turned discs that were to be placed under electrical switches at the Magadan communications office. I fashioned 10,000 discs in 28 days. I got a disability certificate from the doctor that excused me from working for three days because of my swollen feet, and then I took out my last pay.

I completed this, the most depressing period of my life, as a Category 5 woodturner.

The cabinetmakers and some of my compatriots, including Evald Turgan, who had flown from Magadan to Seymchan just for this occasion, came to the airport to see me off. "You'll certainly cry for joy when you see your homeland again!" said the Russian cabinetmaker Zolotarjev, with whom I had worked side-by-side. As I approached my homeland after two weeks of travel, I did not recall my brother cabinetmaker's words until I reached the Petseri station, but because this was no longer the border of my homeland, the man's words simply seemed odd. Only when I heard about the misery and poverty my wife and children had suffered during the eight long years of my absence did I begin to cry. They had been dealt a punishment worse than mine. And for what?

The flight from Seymchan to Khabarovsk took nine hours. I got the last ticket in a non-compartmented car for the evening train from Khabarovsk to Moscow and set off on my trip as a free man.

Soon I got to know my traveling companions, and God provided me the opportunity to continue evangelizing in that train car for all the fifteen days it took to get to Moscow. From there, after standing in line for eight hours to check my hand baggage and for three hours to get my ticket punched, I was so tired that I slept all the way from Moscow to the Estonian border.

As I disembarked the train from Moscow, I noticed a tall boy standing on the platform at Tartu Station. I walked past him. Wanting to travel to Tallinn on the following day, I went to get my ticket punched by the Tartu stationmaster, who recognized me. Two women in front of the station put their heads together and whispered something to each other; they too had recognized me. However, my own son had not recognized me, nor had I recognized him. In eight years, the five-year-old child had grown into a lanky young man.

I went to the St. Paul's congregation office because I could not think of anywhere else to go. It was there that I met this same young man. "Uncle, are you my father?" he asked, turning toward me with an astonished expression. Could I have held back my tears then? He took my hand and did not let go, even as we went to sleep.

After that, I started looking for my family members. I got them all back. God had preserved them, but the misery they had endured during my absence had left a deep mark on their character.

I gathered them together in Tartu, where a colleague of mine gave us two rooms of his former apartment; he had taken great pains with its restoration. We had nothing with which to furnish our abode.

The court ruling had not prescribed confiscation of my belongings, but the Security Special Committee had removed all my things as derelict property, and whatever they had not taken a liking to, they had sold for a pittance.

We started our life again with nothing more than trust in God's grace. And God has truly carried us through everything! Glory to His name!

After suffering for a month due to the change in climate, I was once again strong enough to think about continuing my life's work.

Archbishop Jaan Kiivit let me choose between two congregations he could assign to me: one in Audru, the other in Tarvastu. Staying in Tartu was out of the question, because I had too many friends there.

My wife chose Tarvastu because it was the hometown of her mother, who awaited a better awakening somewhere in the soil of faraway Siberia. Her grandfather had been a loyal church elder at Tarvastu who never let his seat in church stand empty.

That is how I became the pastor of the Tarvastu congregation. I was inducted by the Consistory on November 18, 1955.

The Archbishop told me that he was sending me to Estonia's worst congregation, because it thought that its religious needs would be adequately served if the pastor from the neighboring parish might come and preach to them once a month!

Two clerics had served there before me, but had been forced to abandon the congregation due to economic hardship. Only Deacon Juhan Kallaste, having no clerical training whatsoever, persisted here for two years without complaint. However, it was then that those people who still cherished the word of God began noticing the congregation's spiritual decline, and they joyously welcomed the arrival of a new pastor in Tarvastu.

The Archbishop thought that I might be able to endure three years in Tarvastu, after which he could put me to work serving a better congregation. But neither he nor any of his successors have succeeded in prying me away from this place. The three years I was promised have become 26 years, and now none of my highly esteemed superiors will even give a thought to promoting or demoting me, an old man. I thank them for the heartfelt congratulations they have extended to me on my special celebration days!

My first contact with Tarvastu had occurred as early as 1929. I had been in Viljandi to organize youth activities. I wanted to eat lunch in the Agrarian Society's cafeteria. I asked a paunchy old man if I could sit at his table. He peered at me curiously for a moment and asked for an introduction by inquiring, "I haven't seen you before. Where are you from?" With pride in representing my home island, I answered, "I'm a man from Saaremaa Island!" "Oh, I know those men. I have two islanders digging ditches for me right now," grunted the old man. "And where do you live?" I asked. "I am the master of a farmstead Tarvastu!" he proclaimed, and he never gave me another glance.

And so I was to realize that this master of Tarvastu regarded me, an islander, as nothing better than a ditch-digger. Later, I never found this Tarvastu farmstead master again, nor did I find many others, because most of them had been deported to Siberia. All that were left were their farmhands and house servants, and likely some ditch-diggers from the islands as well. These were the people whose religious needs I was now assigned to attend to.

All right, if God wants to make use of me, then why not in Tarvastu.

The first thing we did was to bring electricity to the church. Then, I began heating the church during the high holidays, something that had not been done since the departure of Pastor Jürmann. Together with the organist, we whitewashed the interior of the church. It was almost by myself that I painted all the church pews and choir lofts, and later the floor as well. In 1978, we had the exterior of the church whitewashed. Indeed, I have not been indifferent toward the congregation that I was sent to serve.

And now, I have become an old man. I give thanks to the Almighty that I have been able to wear myself out in service to his Kingdom! And yet there is still so much more that needs to be done...

I am sure that those who hear the call, as I did, will continue this work, perhaps not in the same way as I have wanted to do and been allowed to do.

I am still standing at my post. God has continued to add days to my life, and I believe it is because I am meant to continue the work He has given me to do, despite my sorry state.

When the Archbishop was here for the 50th anniversary of my ordination, he did not tell me that I have toiled enough. Instead, he expressed the opinion that God might actually give me strength to continue sowing the good seed for several more years in the hope that it will bear fruit.

I know that people are praying for me and my work. Praying for me above all is my wife, who has been my most loyal helpmate in finding joy as we have trod this long road, and also my children and grandchildren.

(Tarvastu, January 21, 1982)

EPILOGUE

Harri Haamer reached Homeland on the 29th of July, 1955. We can only imagine how beautiful the summer there looked to him after eight years in the bleakness of life above the Arctic Circle. Harri immediately started to gather together his scattered family. With his son Andres, he went to find his daughter Maarja and then came for his wife Maimu, for me, and for his foster son Albert. He found us on August 9th in a forest village in South Estonia, where we were hiding from the authorities. For many of the eight years he was in the slave labor camps we had no idea that Father was still alive, so our reunion was one of unspeakable joy. He also had had no way of knowing that any of us had survived, since Soviet murder or starvation had touched nearly every Estonian family.

We left for Tartu, where we had been living before Father's imprisonment. Now it was possible to return in public, because the harsh policy had changed and people were not punished as before. Stalin was dead, and the people who had escaped from deportation to Siberia were not chased any more. Later, life became harder again, however, as Communist leaders changed.

Soon after having returned to his homeland, Father fell gravely ill. We were worried and fearful that his time might be over, since he was weak and thin. Mother prayed for God to give us ten more years to be together, and her prayer was heard. We were blessed with many more years together with him.

In that autumn, Father was appointed to serve the small congregation at Tarvastu, because he was not allowed to work for his previous congregation at St. Paul Church in Tartu. The Communist authorities were afraid to let him stay in Tartu, which is the university town, as they feared his Christian influence on the students there.

So it was that on the last Sunday of the Church Year in 1955 Father celebrated his first service. It had been a long time since he had led his people in worship. Before the Soviet occupation there had been a huge congregation at Tarvastu of over 10,000 members, but now only about 300 remained. The members of this congregation had been prosperous farmers, but most of them had been deported to Siberia with their families and had died there. My father was deliberately appointed to this very small congregation, to avoid his "spoiling people with faith."

My mother stood beside him in his work; they worked faithfully for God's Kingdom in this small congregation and never complained. Both Mother and Father were fond of singing and they passed on this love of singing to their offspring. We are happy to have a recording of their songs.

At Tarvastu, Father wrote a lot. He wrote down his sermons and commentary on many books of the Bible: The Epistle of Paul to the Ephesians, original stories in the Bible, Abraham's story, the books of Jeremiah, Lamentations, Ecclesiastes, Ezekiel, and several more. His works were mainly explaining and clarifying the Bible, as well as evangelizing the readers.

It was also at Tarvastu that he wrote down his memoirs from Siberia, but during the Soviet occupation he had to hide the manuscript that has become this book, *We Shall Live in Heaven*. If the authorities had found it, he might have been sent to Siberia once more. The Soviet secret police (KGB) harassed him a lot. The police were disturbed by young people gathering in my parents' home, because my father had a great religious influence on them. Father knew how to communicate with young people. He was also a popular speaker in underground young Christian camps.

Father was a very active man as well as an assiduous and fearless propagator of Christianity. He liked to ride bicycle and considered sports as an important lifestyle.

Father was very pleased that I also chose to be a pastor. He dearly loved his family, and my wife and I and our children were happy to visit my parents, as were my siblings' families, so our children got direction for their lives from them. He loved to play with his grandchildren, and they all loved him very much.

He wrote a book for each of his grandchildren on their fifth birthday. All of these stories have been gathered together and published (in Estonian) as faith-building readings for children. Two books of father's sermons have also been published in Estonian, but there are so many of his sermons that several books could still be published. His sermons are very easy to read, and people like them because he preached as if he was speaking directly to his listeners. However, it was not possible to publish any of his works until Estonia gained its independence in 1991, four years after his death.

His time on earth was over in the evening of August 8, 1987, as the Lord invited His faithful servant home. Father had just celebrated his 81st birthday on the 8th of July. He had a healthy mind with an extraordinary memory until the end. A doctor who talked with him not long before he passed away later told us that he had not felt that he was talking to a dying person.

The Lord had given him nearly 33 years to be with his family after his return from Siberia. His funeral took place on the 14th of August, and about 2,000 people gathered to say farewell to him. We were able to see that he really was greatly honored and beloved. His funeral was the first public manifestation of the Estonian people's anti-Soviet feelings during the period of their occupation. This large crowd went from the church to the cemetery on foot, a distance of a mile and a half, singing songs of faith. Such an action was strictly forbidden and punishable at that time.

Thank God Father did not die in Siberia, nor did he live his life in emptiness or in vain. He is still always remembered with gratitude.

Blessed be his memory!

Eenok Haamer
Harri's elder son

Want support education of Estonian clergy and pastoral care givers?

If you would like to make a donation to support mission work and the education of clergy and pastoral care givers in Estonia you are welcome to find options from tatest.org.

CHRONOLOGY

Harri Haamer was born on July 8, 1906 in the town of Kuressaare as the second son of Caroline-Juliane and Aleksander Haamer.

In 1922, he gave his Boy Scout oath. Later, he became one of the leaders of the Estonian Boy Scout movement.

In 1924, he graduated from the Kuressaare Upper Secondary School.

In 1924, he entered the Tartu University School of Divinity.

On December 24, 1925, he conducted his first service at the age of 19 in the Elva church.

In 1928, he graduated from Tartu University.

In 1929, he served as Youth Organization secretary until his ordination.

On October 6, 1929, he was ordained and sent to Saaremaa to serve the Püha congregation.

In 1933, he was selected to be pastor of the Tartu St. Paul congregation.

On May 10, 1934, he married Maimu Maramaa.

On February 4, 1948, he was arrested.

On July 29, 1955, he returned to his homeland.

Since November 18, 1955, he has been pastor of the Tarvastu congregation.

Starting in 1962, he gave lectures on the Old Testament at the Theological Institute until he was relieved of his position at the demand of the Soviet security apparatus.

Starting in 1964, he served without pay as pastor of the Kõpu congregation as well. This double assignment endured for 17 years.

On August 8, 1987, God called his loyal servant to join him in the Eternal Kingdom.

"We shall live in heaven" was his favorite saying, and it is inscribed onto his headstone.

GLOSSARY

Banderas – Nickname given to people from Western Ukraine
Batja – "Father," a term Russians used for all clergy; perhaps said in derision
Batyushka – Father, bishop, Patriarch; common usage for Orthodox clergy
blackcoat – Clergyman; a derogatory reference to traditional clerical garb
buri – Isolation cell; unheated and with open windows; rations were bread and water
chekist – Communist secret police agent (KGB)
chifir – Very, very potent fermented tea
"cow" to be "milked" – A prisoner placed into each cell as a snitch; the authorities would periodically remove him from the cell so that he could tell them about what was being said and done there
dobre – Ukrainian for "good"
freiers – Non-thieves; prisoners because of their political beliefs or faith
fufaika – Quilted jacket; a prisoner or ex-prisoner dressed in one
gold-epaulette – Shoulder fringes on Communist Youth uniforms; this signified a higher rank
gymnastiorka – Soldier's blouse-type shirt; typical of long, belted slipover peasant tops
KGB – Soviet secret police; spies and enforcers of the Communist state
Komsomol – Young Communist League; membership was required of all young people
konvoi – Convoy guard
kormushka – "Fodder bin" the hole through which prisoners were fed.

Korpusnoi – Prison unit commander
kulak – Farmer; term used to vilify those who would not give away their land to collective farms
Maiki – Pastor Haamer's nickname for his wife Maimu
makhorka – Cheap tobacco
muzhiki – Group of men; men in general; peasants
otboi – "Down for the night!": an order that all the men must be on the bunks
parask – Latrine bucket; usually a barrel crudely cut in half
patronymic – Middle name; shows father's name; "Mikailovich," son of Mikail
pridurka – A trusty, or political prisoner who sides with the regime for rank and other perks
red-epaulette – Shoulder fringes on Communist Youth uniforms; this signified a lower rank
Sanpropusk – Sanitation entrance
s vestsami – "With your things;" an order for a prisoner to move out
SS officer – Special police unit in Hitler's army
Section 10 – "Law" forbidding "propaganda and agitation Article 28 against the USSR" under which Stalin imprisoned Christians and others who did not follow his beliefs
Stakhanovite – Legendary, celebrated hard worker in communist countries; muscular icon portrayed on billboards and in films
suka – Criminal prisoners who collaborate with the Communists
taiga – A vast coniferous forest in the far north
three-striper – Arm-patch of a sergeant; more advanced rank in the Soviet army
two-striper – Arm patch of a mid-ranking officer in the Soviet army
urkas – Professional thieves who terrorize and rob other prisoners
white night – Special light of long summer evenings in Arctic regions
yest – "I'm here"

Landscape of Kolyma. Painted by Harri Haamer 1960.

Labor camp in Kolyma. Painted by Harri Haamer 1960.

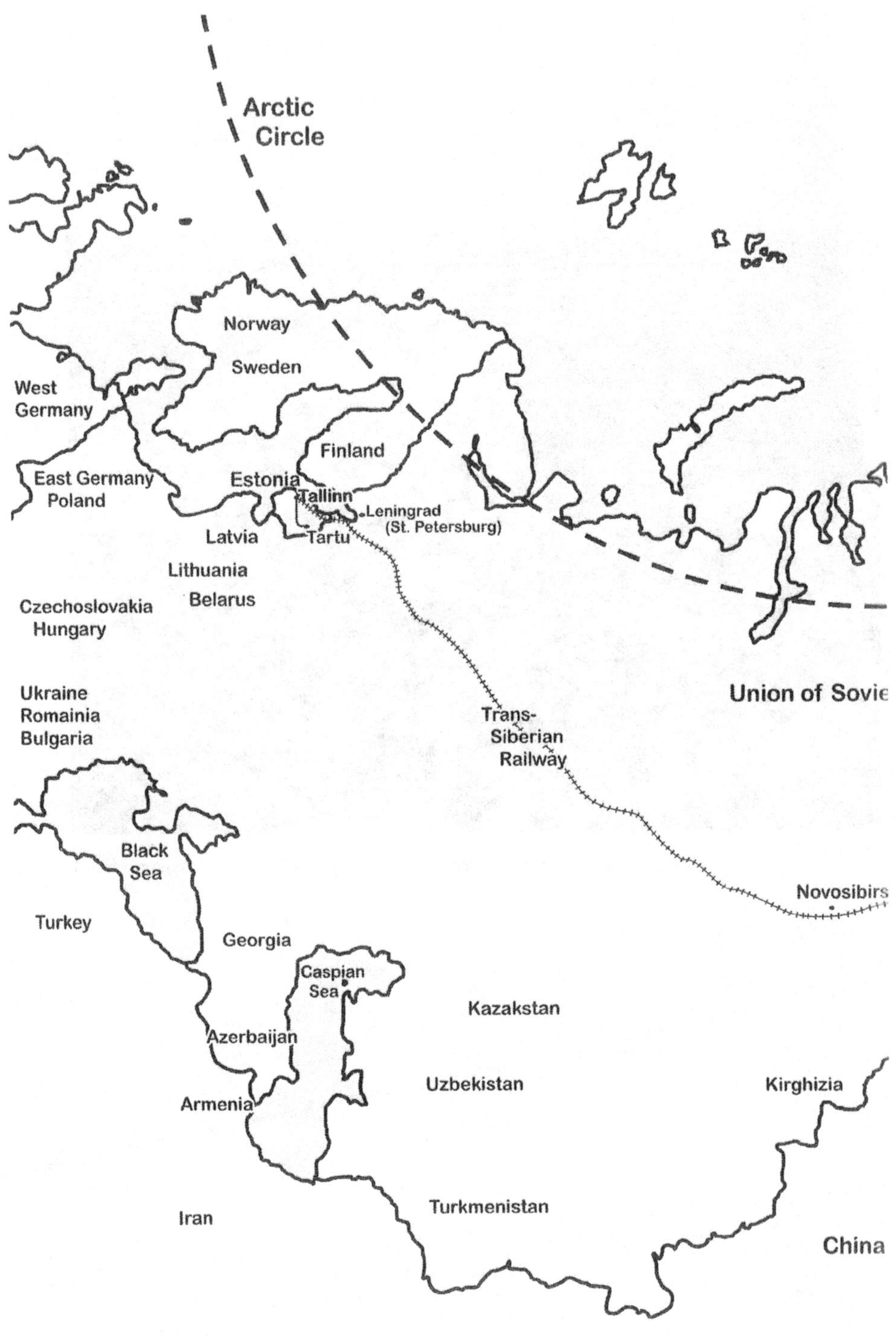
Arctic Circle
Norway
Sweden
West Germany
Finland
East Germany
Poland
Estonia
Tallinn
Leningrad (St. Petersburg)
Latvia
Tartu
Lithuania
Belarus
Czechoslovakia
Hungary
Ukraine
Romainia
Bulgaria
Union of Sovie
Trans-Siberian Railway
Black Sea
Novosibirs
Turkey
Georgia
Caspian Sea
Kazakstan
Azerbaijan
Uzbekistan
Kirghizia
Armenia
Turkmenistan
Iran
China
Afghanistan

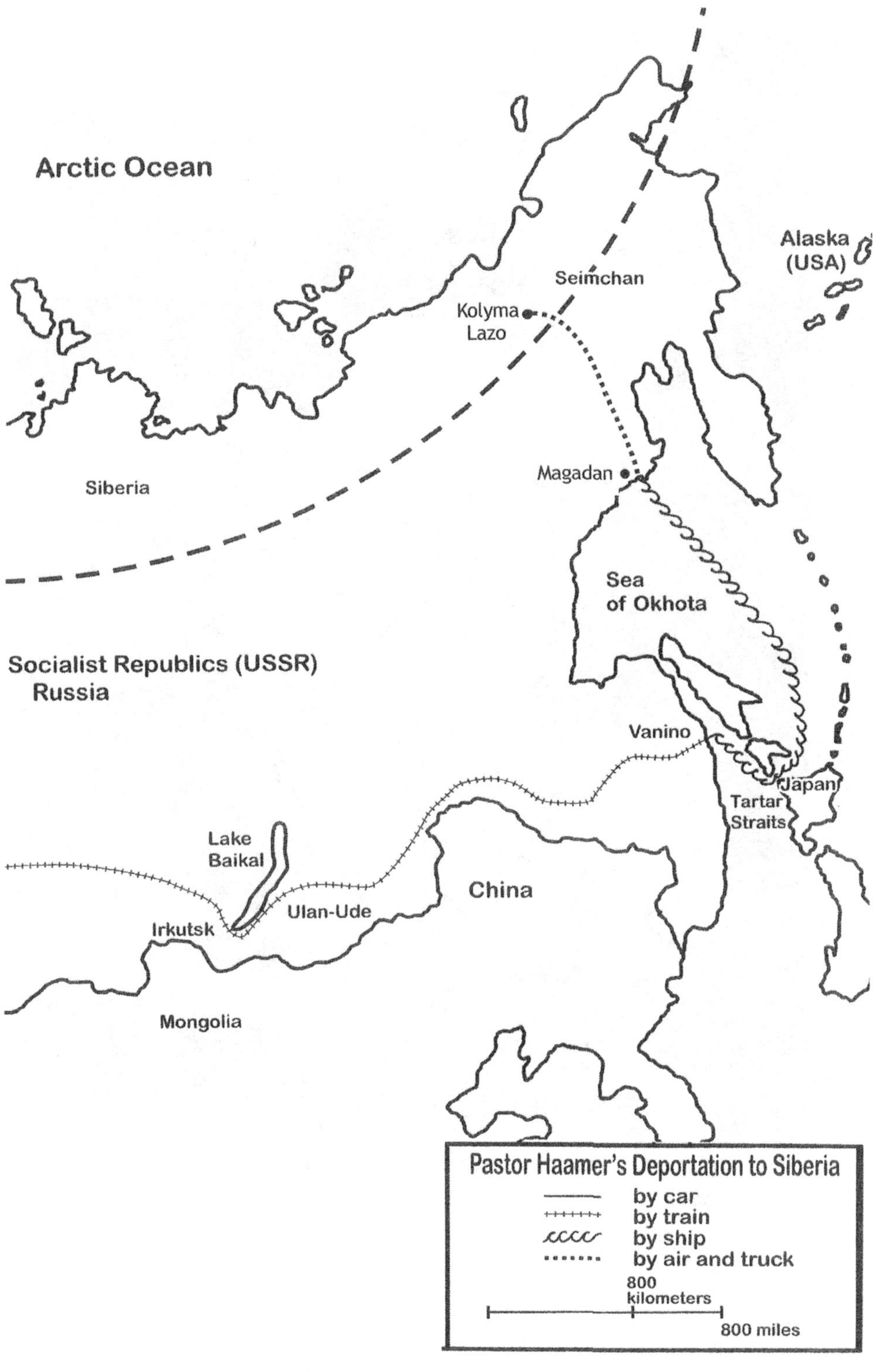
Arctic Ocean
Alaska
(USA)
Seimchan
Kolyma
Lazo
Magadan
Siberia
Sea
of Okhota
Socialist Republics (USSR)
Russia
Vanino
Japan
Tartar
Straits
Lake
Baikal
China
Ulan-Ude
Irkutsk
Mongolia
Pastor Haamer's Deportation to Siberia
by car
by train
by ship
by air and truck
800
kilometers
800 miles

Harri and Maimu Haamer with their children Eenok, Maarja and Andres, Spring 1947.

The family together again in 1955 after Harri was allowed to return from Siberia.
l-r: Andres, Maimu, Harri, Maarja, Eenok, foster son Albert.

Harri Haamer while in exile in Kolyma 1955.

Harri Haamer going to church on his bysicle, November 1986.

3 generations of pastors. Taken in front of altar at Tarvastu Church July 14, 1987.
l-r: Markus, Eenok, Harri and Naatan. (A third grandson, Siimon, is also pastor)